HARVARD MIDDLE EASTERN MONOGRAPHS

IX

NORTH AFRICA'S FRENCH LEGACY
1954–1962

BY

DAVID C. GORDON

DISTRIBUTED FOR THE
CENTER FOR MIDDLE EASTERN STUDIES
OF HARVARD UNIVERSITY BY
HARVARD UNIVERSITY PRESS
CAMBRIDGE, MASSACHUSETTS
1964

Second Printing, 1964

LIBRARY OF CONGRESS CATALOG CARD NUMBER 62–21836

PRINTED IN THE UNITED STATES OF AMERICA

PREFACE

This survey of the cultural relationship between France and the North African nations of Morocco, Tunisia, and Algeria since the Second World War was completed in the first part of 1962 while I was on a research grant at the Center for Middle Eastern Studies at Harvard University. My interest in this topic is the product of many years spent among Arab intellectuals in Lebanon, a visit to North Africa in the summer of 1960, and my interest in French history both as student and teacher. My conclusions are inevitably tentative and of an evocative and suggestive, rather than of a "scientific," nature. Material was derived from a wide variety of sources including interviews, both formal and informal, novels, newspapers and periodicals, as well as from the basic secondary sources. Statistics have been made use of where they were available, but impression and intuition have played an important role. So also has my sympathy for both French culture and Arab self-determination.

I am grateful for the help and advice of many, especially of Mrs. Forrest Crawford, William Gresham, Arthur Close, Taha Ben Hamida, Miss Margaret Pope, Paul Teyssier, and Charles Gallagher. Professor A. J. Meyer, Associate Director of the Center for Middle Eastern Studies, has also been very helpful, as have Miss Carol Cross, Miss Brenda Sens, and Miss Elizabeth Randolph of the Center office. Generous financial assistance was provided by the Committee on Research at the American University of Beirut and by the Harvard Center for Middle Eastern Studies.

This book is for Ann, Victoria, and Matthew.

DAVID C. GORDON

Cambridge, Massachusetts
July, 1962

CONTENTS

NORTH AFRICA'S FRENCH LEGACY
1954–1962

The former *Président du Conseil* Edgar Faure tells how during the discussion of the Moroccan agreements he received two delegations in the same day: the first consisted of Moroccans wearing jallabahs and babushes, speaking French with difficulty, and loudly and sincerely insisting that the French remain in the realm of the *sherif*. The second was composed of elegant gentlemen in European clothes and speaking impeccable French, all graduates of our universities and our institutes: it had come to express to the head of the state the sentiments of unyielding nationalism on the part of the Moroccan elite which France had formed.

(Jean Bloch-Michel)

J'y fis des études littéraires, et même du latin. J'y fis aussi l'expérience d'un enseignement étranger, qui je le sentais, m'éloignait de mon milieu familial, de ma religion, de mon passé. Nous essayions tous, nous les Tunisiens, de compenser. Mes camarades étaient musulmans, pas français. Je redoutais une coupure avec mon pays. Pourtant aujourd'hui je dois reconnaître que je lis plus volontiers le français que l'arabe littéraire, que je goute Rousseau mais pas Ibn Zeidoun, que je connais mal l'histoire des Beni Hillal et celle des Aghlabites.

(A graduate of the Lycée Carnot in Tunis)

I

INTRODUCTION

Shortly before his death in the summer of 1961, Frantz Fanon, a prophet of African and more particularly of Algerian anti-colonialism, published *Les damnés de la terre*.[1] In it he implored his fellow Africans to repudiate all vestiges of their colonial legacy, cultural as well as economic and political. He insisted that the rejection of the West must be radical and even violent. Only through revolution, and only through the refusal to solve social and economic difficulties in cooperation with a previous colonizer, could the African discover his identity and cease to be among the damned of the earth. On the cultural level, he maintained, Africa should reject the individualistic and rationalistic legacy of Greece and Rome and return to a communalist tradition that was once its own, and he denounced all Western-educated Africans who refused to unite with the masses of their peoples in revolution and in a repudiation of the "narcissistic egoism" of the West.

It is with some of these Westernized Africans whom Fanon so bitterly denounced that the present book is concerned, with their dilemmas, their aspirations, and their policies as the elites of newly independent countries. The Westernized elites to be considered are those of Tunisia, Morocco, and Algeria, the three Arab North African nations whose experience of the West, before, during and after independence, has been France. A question underlying this book is whether the French-educated class that now largely rules in Tunisia and Morocco and which in the main has directed the Algerian revolution for independence is to be condemned by history, as Fanon would have it, or whether it will be able to integrate, in new cultural forms, the legacy of the Arabs with the heritage of the French colonial past. The emphasis will be upon the "dialogue," to use a favorite French term, between the French-educated Arab North African and France. The period to be considered covers roughly the years from the beginning of the Algerian revolution in 1954 to July 1962. By this time Morocco and Tunisia had experienced five years of independence and Algeria had largely been molded in the crucible of warfare. The French-Moslem dialogue has its beginning in the imposition of the French presence. It continues with the growing self-awareness on the part of the Westernized Arab of the indignity of his status, of his cultural uprootedness, and also of the backwardness of his nation by Western standards. It takes new forms with independence in ways that can only be surmised and hoped for.

A characteristic feature of French colonialism since the nineteenth century has been the policy of educating native elites to speak and think like Frenchmen. This policy of cultural assimilation is motivated by two considerations. The one is ethnocentric — to dominate. The other is generous and progressive — to liberate. The French purpose has been to bind these French-educated elites to metropolitan France through ties of sentiment and loyalty, and so to perpetuate French political influence both before and after independence. But the intention has also been to spread to less "civilized" parts of the world the culture that many Frenchmen believe to be one of the highest, if not the highest, expression of human civilization. It is revealing that the term the French use for a French-educated native is *évolué*.[2] This term has no English equivalent. The *évolué* is the person who has literally evolved from a lower state of existence to a higher one after adopting the French language, French dress, and French ways. An implication of the term is that the person to whom it is applied has become not only French enculturated, but also civilized. The notion dies hard with many Frenchmen, and also with many of the *évolués* they have trained, that there are alternative and equally valuable kinds of civilizations other than that of Europe and of France in particular. André Malraux once suggested that France has only just awakened to the fact that her culture is no longer universal.

In the tumultuous days that have followed the Second World War, the bulk of the peoples once ruled by European powers have obtained their independence. The European empires of the pre-war period are rapidly disappearing, and the French empire, in particular, has become an institution of the past. Yet for a long time to come those who rule former French subjects will know the cultural imprint of France, use her language, and reflect her culture. And the French policy of cultural radiation will continue where it still can in the form of what France's critics are wont to term "neo-colonialism."

It is paradoxical but not strange that many of the North African leaders have revolted against France in the name of French values and French revolutionary principles, rather than in the name of the values of their own traditional culture. Such *évolués*, deeply imbued with the culture of France and sometimes educated to speak only in the French language, have revolted without losing their love for France or their respect for the French cultural legacy in North Africa. The image of the Algerian rebel yearning for peace so that he might revisit Paris is not completely frivolous. But at the same time these French-educated nationalists have revolted against France because of the very fact that France has made them strangers to their own nation. They are caught in the dilemma, often, of admiring that which they condemn.

In many North African cities there is a clear separation between the "native quarter" (the *medina*) and the modern city the French have built by its side, the "new city," as it is termed. This duality can be taken to symbolize the schism French domination produced in the life and the psyche of North Africa.[3] The *évolué* who lives most comfortably in the "new city" wishes to open this city to the mass of his people once excluded from it. At the same time he wishes to bridge the gulf that separated him from the people of the *medina*. His hope often is to unite his country culturally and to integrate his own French culture with the traditional heritage of Islam. He resents the extent to which France disparaged this traditional Islamic culture and sought to frustrate its development, and he deplores the degree to which he himself has been divorced, because of his French education, from this traditional culture. In Morocco and Tunisia, both independent since 1956, there has been a natural attempt to educate the youth in traditional culture and in the Arabic language. But at the same time there has been a reluctance to abandon the heritage of the culture and language of France which was the medium through which most of the North African leaders entered the twentieth century. The *évolué* of North Africa remains ambivalent in his attitudes toward the problem of cultural decolonization. It is not inevitable that North Africa will become as monolingual as the Arab East or will abandon its dialogue with France and so with the West. However, the understanding and sympathy that sustain dialogue must be mutual.

II

THE *MISSION CIVILISATRICE*

In 1930 the Governor-General of French West Africa boasted that the peoples of his territory were developing "a closer yet wider contact with French life and institutions through the diffusion of the French language; and the establishment, as circumstances offer, of a native *élite*, of whose zeal for a thorough and exclusively French culture signs are already visible." [1] The aim of the French, suggested by this statement, to spread their culture overseas has been the characteristic cultural policy of the French, their version of the "white man's burden." This policy has not been, of course, the major motive of French colonialism, but it has been a major feature of the expression and conduct of this colonialism. It is a policy that has been carried out with determination and with considerable success. It is not strange that an observer should be more struck by the differences between the French- and British-educated African elites, for example, than by their similarities as Africans. Herbert Passin points this up in a perceptive description of a seminar sponsored by the Congress for Cultural Freedom in Ibadan, Nigeria. [2] He found the French-speaking Africans sounding like "an editorial in *France-Observateur*" while the English speakers were "sober and commonsensical." The French-trained were astonished to see tribal chiefs in their regalia ("c'est un vrai musée vivant. . . ." said one French-speaking intellectual); they were much less interested in the continuance of traditional ways than were the English speakers; they seldom wore native dress; in sum, the author found "a profound difference in styles of thought" between the two elites.

The success that the French have had in enculturating native elites is the product of an unusual self-confidence and pride in their own culture. [3] Theirs has been an energetic and dedicated application of a uniform and centralized system of education to other parts of the world — often with indifference or hostility — to alter native pre-existing cultural patterns. This effort has been and is inspired by a fervor that almost suggests a cultural crusade. A typical French saying once was: "When the Portuguese colonized, they built churches; when the British colonized, they built trading stations; when the French colonize, they build schools." [4]

The French system of education is democratic through the first four years of secondary school (when the student is about fifteen), after which it is highly selective, competitive, and even aristocratic throughout the system of higher education. Thus in the first years, education is intended to provide literacy and a general body of knowledge to all the people, and in the later years the intention is to train a specialized elite.

In the first part of the student's education, up through the *baccalauréat* degrees, parts one and two, the French program is general and humanistic. (The age of the student who takes the *baccalauréat* ranges from fifteen to eighteen.) The next degree, the *licence*, and all higher degrees are obtained after specialized training. Administratively, French education is highly centralized. All curricula, both public and private, must conform to specifications set by the Ministry of Education, and examinations, intended to serve as eliminatory hurdles, are set for all French students by this Ministry. Educational France is one university. French education emphasizes clarity in thought and expression and the ability of the student to synthesize and analyze. Considerable stress is laid upon philosophy and logical deduction, and until the Second World War secondary schooling was heavily classical and tended to concentrate upon memorization and the verbal, deductive, literary side of education as opposed to the more practical and experimental approach of the American system. Since the war, greater emphasis is being placed upon technical training; the amount of mathematics and science in the secondary program has been increased, and in history less emphasis is being placed upon memorization and more emphasis upon the analysis of documents and general understanding. The French know that competition in the modern world of rapid scientific and technological advance requires educational reform. They are aware that not since 1935 has a single Nobel prize in science been awarded to a Frenchman. But they can still boast that a plurality of recent Nobel prize winners in literature have been French moralist writers who have defended the ideal of human sanctity in an age of mass conformism and totalitarianism. The French still regard their system of educa-

tion as a superior medium for the training of the intellect and for
inculcating into the student the values of human dignity and
national pride.[5]

It is through their system of education that the French have
introduced abroad their values and something of their style, that
mixture of Gallic wit, irritability, and concern for what is correct,
measured, and reasonable (the sense of *droit*). The colonized have
taken to this process of frenchification in different degrees, of
course, and today, when nationalism sweeps the non-European
world, they have judged the French system and reacted to it in a
variety of ways. Educated Moslem Arabs tend to be ambivalent
in their evaluation of the contribution that the French system has
made to the development of their own people. Some criticisms
that have been made by Arab educators are the following: the
French system emphasizes the alien French language, culture, and
history to the neglect of native language, culture, and history; it
emphasizes intellectualism and memorization and it fosters verbal-
ism; it fails to attend to the extra-curricular development of the
"whole man" and to bring him into close and critical contact with
his environment (in France this side of the student's life is handled
by the Church and by movements like the Boy Scouts); and the
French system has not until recently placed enough stress upon
modern technology and science. Thus Dr. Habib Kurani, long-
time head of the Department of Education at the American University of Beirut, criticizes education in Syria under the French
mandate in the following terms: "Education remained theoretical.
Secondary education was emphasized. Curricula were inspired by
foreign ideas and were overloaded with book knowledge empha-
sizing memory. Vocational and practical education was inadequate. Elementary education was conceived essentially as a prepa-
ration for academic secondary education without useful knowledge."[6] On the other hand, many Arabs would agree that the
French system is superior to anything that had come before, that
it did train the student remarkably well in the French language,
and that it did educate the student in logical thought and expression. The author has talked to Arabs who are fervent defenders of
the French system and who believe it still provides the finest
humanistic training in the world and is bearer of the highest
expression of Western humanistic culture.

Many Frenchmen involved in the colonial adventure, in any
case, have been convinced of both the superiority and universality

of their culture, and of its educational medium of distribution. They have felt justified in isolating, ignoring, or even undermining cultural patterns of peoples they have dominated. In this respect, they are more rigid and perhaps more proud than their British or American counterparts. Often convinced that by making French education a possibility for the native-born they are being generous and progressive, Frenchmen tend to disparage or to combat those elements in the culture of the conquered people which offer resistance to the *mission civilisatrice.* They do so with sincerity. And in Africa, the most serious opposition to this mission has been Islam, a religion and a culture with a rich heritage. Moslems have not been wholly incorrect in believing that many Frenchmen, though certainly not scholars like Louis Massignon and Charles-André Julien, harbor, consciously or not, a tendency to disparage and to condemn Islam. Islam, for example, is often considered to be the cause of Arab "decadence." A classical articulation of this view was Renan's in an address to the Sorbonne in March 1883 [7] in which he belittled the medieval contribution of Islam and blamed Islam for the suppression of the spirit of intellectual and philosophical inquiry. Georges Hardy, director of the French Colonial School in Paris, has described Islam as a religion that feeds on xenophobia and fanaticism.[8] Where it is strong, Islam should be tolerated, he has written, but never encouraged; nor should it be treated as a higher religion. John Trimingham describes French policy toward Moslems in Africa south of the Sahara as one of training elites to be assimilated and so cut off from their tribal origins.[9] Shortly before World War I, he observes, the French began to discourage Islam — the belief was that it constituted a threat to the civilizing mission; controls were placed upon the collecting of alms, itinerant preaching, the founding of mosques, and pilgrimages. And a prominent French educator in North Africa could write (in 1923): "To liberate the Moslem populations from the prejudices that separate them from our civilization and to raise their moral and intellectual level, France has no more effective a means than primary education." [10]

The French, in relative contrast to the British, have also been inflexible in face of growing nationalism among colonial peoples. George Kirk quotes Pierre Rondot to this effect.[11]

For a long time we ignored Arab nationalism. As it was often the expression of young lawyers and publicists, the product of our schools, we tended to regard it as a pure verbal exercise. . . . The powerful echo that nationalism was to find in the masses, thanks in particular to the interpenetration of Arab and Moslem sentiment, was not sufficiently felt, or at least was not appreciated at its proper value, in French administrative circles. The men in those offices, however benevolent, tended to contrast the dreams of the intellectuals with the positive preoccupations of cultivators and traders. They did not imagine what their effect would be on the subconscious emotional level. . . .

The frequent failure of the French colonial administrators to assess correctly the depth of anti-colonial sentiment has had tragic consequences in the present age of decolonization. In Indo-China, the Levant, and in North Africa, France has forfeited much good will and influence that she might have retained. "What loyalties wasted," Gilbert Grandval, one of the few enlightened Resident-Generals of Morocco, once remarked, "what genuine friendships placed in doubt and rejected by the French whose clairvoyance does not equal their patriotism!" [12] But it has not only been her lack of perspicacity that has caused France so many difficulties in the post-World War II period. France has also suffered because she clung for so long to a vision of herself and of her destiny which has been brave and grand, but also quixotic and, in the twentieth century, obsolete. This has been the vision of France as the heir to ancient Rome, in a large part of the globe, as the bearer of the so-called *mission civilisatrice*.

Herbert Luethy has described the French sense of mission succinctly and usefully, although somewhat too categorically, in a passage in his *France Against Herself*. Allowance should be made today, of course, for the fact that this was written before the French Community (a type of commonwealth) came into being. Luethy writes: [13]

All French ideologies meet and harmonize in the idea of a greater France of "A hundred million Frenchmen." It has the true French *élan*, and combines the French love of a resounding phrase with the hard French spirit of realism; it is humanitarian in spirit, takes into account the military necessity of recruiting, and at the same time implies that subtle form of "dividing and ruling" which consists of setting up a privileged and assimilated *élite* over against the primitive masses and thus depriving the latter of their natural leaders. It provides common ground for the egalitarian idealism of the Jacobins and the Christian missionary ideal of the *ancien régime*, the worldly and the religious form of that "imperialism in its civilizing role" which is inseparable from the French national idea; in short, it envisages a whole great section of humanity on the march to absorption by France, the civilized nation *par excellence*.

A perusal of the writings of leading prophets of modern French

imperialism reveals the importance placed upon cultural assimi
tion. Leroy-Beaulieu, a leading spokesman of colonialism in t.
nineteenth century, flatly stated that ". . . the way to dominate
a people is to assimilate it, to seize the youth in its infancy. . . .
The knowledge of the Koran is disappearing in Algeria; it must
not be revived; it is a book full of bellicose exhortations against
infidels and includes thousands of texts that can be used against
us. . . ." [14] "North Africa," he added, "will only belong to us
definitively if we conciliate the Arabs and, to a certain extent,
frenchify them." As examples of successful domination by the
French, he cited the Bretons, the Flemish, and the Alsatians. And
more recently, in a standard work on Algeria, Augustin Bernard,
an old colonial hand, stated: "Our final goal, conforming to our
ideal of yesterday and today, the ideal of Richelieu and of Louis
XIV as well as of the French Revolution, is the foundation of a
France Overseas where our language and civilization [will be
established] with the collaboration, more and more close of the
natives and of the French, in one word by their frenchification." [15]

The origin of this sense of mission to assimilate is a matter of
dispute, but its roots and anticipations go back to periods of
French grandeur, periods when it was not so absurd to have identified civilization with its French expression: the Crusades which
were largely manned by Frenchmen; the age of Louis XIV when
French became the language of the cultivated European and when
Descartes was interpreted to say that all men had in common
reason with which they could attain to the same and single universal truth (implied, the possibility of assimilation); or the period
of the Enlightenment and its fruit the French Revolution, when
Robespierre could say (speech of May 15, 1790): "It is in the
interest of all nations to protect the French nation because it is
from France that liberty and the happiness of the world will
come." In 1848 Lamartine saw France as the model the rest of the
world would follow to form "that great intellectual nation which
will be the completion of the French Revolution and the establishment of international fraternity on the globe." And, in 1875
Victor Hugo could write: "Greece was transformed to become
the Christian world; France will transfigure herself to become
the human world." [16]

Whatever the sources of the civilizing mission of France, the
reality of it in contemporary history is evident. French scholars
of French colonialism readily admit that this crusading and

assimilationist tendency has been characteristic of the French colonial venture.[17] René Maunier in his sociological study of colonialism states: "It was the French who, in the last century, at the time of their conquest of Algeria, first expressed the idea of assimilation properly so called, by means of education, the idea of propagating civilization." [18] And Robert Montagne, an expert on Morocco, felt that General Lyautey's plan to preserve as much autonomy and native culture in Morocco as possible was undermined by his successors because: "[His plan] made no place for the assimilatory tendencies, those tendencies so powerful in the minds of our French elites, generous when it comes to diffusing culture and reticent when the consequences of progress realized through contact with us, presents itself on a political plane." [19] And an American student of Indo-China writes in the same vein: "Developments in French colonial policy after 1850 illustrate this persistent urge to enhance national prestige and to vindicate French cultural superiority. . . . For many imperialist apologists in France, no boon to be conferred on colonial protégés in Annam could match being transformed into brown-skinned Frenchmen. . . ." [20]

The policy of complete cultural assimilation has been the French ideal, but realities inevitably forced France to compromise with this ideal. The usual policy she has adopted has been that of "association," particularly since the turn of the century.[21] This policy, as Eric Walker describes it in his comparative study of colonization, "aims at transferring a native élite into Frenchmen, and leaves the masses to learn enough French for workaday purposes, and, if all goes well, to earn a better living than they have done hitherto." [22] Thus the policy of association has been a compromise with the policy of assimilation, not a rejection of it. The culture to be imposed upon colonial territories was to remain exclusively French to the extent that such an imposition was possible. One purpose of concentrating upon the elites of the colonial territories was, of course, to assure that the natural leaders of the colonies would feel sentimentally tied to metropolitan France and as a result prove to be politically loyal to France. In contrast to Great Britain, which has encouraged her colonies to evolve toward self-government, French policy has been centripetal. It has aimed at developing the colonies economically and politically in terms of the interests of metropolitan France, and, until the post-World War II period, it has rejected the idea of native self-government. Since 1945 circumstances have forced France to change her political policy, and today the French empire has evolved through the Union (something of a disguise for the continuation of the old system) to the present amorphous Community, and the old protectorates of Morocco and Tunisia as well as many of the sub-Sahara states have become fully independent.

But although France has now abandoned the principle of metropolitan control of the colonies politically, it continues to support and encourage the spread of its culture and to view this culture as an important investment overseas. The assumption that the French make is that they will enjoy some degree of political influence in those newly independent nations which remain within the sphere of France's cultural radiation. Typically, in a newspaper item in *Le Monde* in September 1959, concern was expressed over the fact that the Secretary of State of National Education of Vietnam had announced that henceforth only one instead of two languages would be required in the cycle of secondary studies.[23] This, the writer stated, constituted a menace to the predominance of the French language in coming years. The title of a long article by Robert Gauthier reads: "Professors and Instructors assure the Permanence of French Culture in Morocco and Tunisia," [24] and in December 1958, an article celebrated the seventy-fifth year of the *Alliance Française*.[25] The author observed that this world-wide institution was founded by men as prominent as Paul Cambon, Paul Bert, Ferdinand de Lesseps, Jusserand and Cardinal Lavigerie. It has as its purpose the promotion in France and abroad of the French language and of French civilization — the *Alliance* offered courses in 1958 to 80,000 students all over the world (5,300 in Buenos Aires, 500 in Calcutta, 400 in Johannesburg).[26]

It is still with energy, and despite her loss of empire, that France pursues her mission. But she does so with some anxiety as well. In Tunis, an American cultural officer stated that in 1960 more students were eager to learn English than could be accommodated by the United States Information Service and the French Cultural Counselor observed that the schools of the French Mission were teaching many students English because of its popularity as a second language; French is no longer the supreme Western language it once was. A casual remark made by a cultivated Tunisian mother has significance for the future; she said that she intended to send her child to America to study because it was there that the most important work was being done in modern science. And in the summer of 1959, Jean Lacouture, *Le Monde*'s correspondent, saw ominous significance in the fact that one of the most powerful figures in contemporary Morocco, Muhammad El-Basri,[27] did not speak French; this was a new phenomenon among an elite which is all French speaking, he observed, and one which did not presage France any good.[28]

In an age of rapid decolonization, then, and in a period when the power and prestige of France have diminished at least relatively, one question confronting the French is how to preserve their cultural presence in areas that they once ruled. In North Africa, conditions have remained somewhat favorable — the French presence still has deep roots — but there have been, and continue to be, pitfalls. The greatest of these has been the Algerian war, which the French only succeeded vainly in ending after almost eight years and which has served to plague and poison her relations with the states of Morocco and Tunisia, as well as with the Arab and African worlds in general. Another pitfall has resulted from the material presence of France in the newly-independent countries — vested economic interests, the garrison in Bizerte, troops in Morocco, and the French *colon* population that remained in these countries and still, in 1962, often possessed the best lands and had a dominant control of the Tunisian and Moroccan economies. The danger has been that the French might jeopardize their cultural influence and prestige by the manner in which they maintained and defended this material presence. A third pitfall has been the political confusion, if not anarchy, which threatened to engulf metropolitan France in 1961–62, as it had in 1958, and which has tended to frustrate many efforts by responsible statesmen to solve the remaining colonial problems of France with wisdom and with vision. And a fourth pitfall lying in an unpredictable future is suggested by Rupert Emerson in his comprehensive study of decolonization: "In the first round of succession the nationalists of the Western school have taken power to themselves and won the allegiance of their people against the encroachments of the alien imperialism. It is not self-evident that they will be able both to maintain their power and to hold firm to their purpose as imperialism recedes and as other aspirants to power challenge their leadership." [29] It is not impossible that a

day might come when the frenchness of the present elites in North
Africa will be regarded as one of the last vestiges of imperialism
or of what is called today neo-colonialism. In the North Africa of
1962, this prospect appeared conceivable, but by no means inevitable.

III

THE FRENCH PRESENCE SIX YEARS AFTER
INDEPENDENCE: TUNISIA AND MOROCCO

In general, the relationship between France and the two North African states of Morocco and Tunisia has been surprisingly good since independence in 1956. The Algerian revolution has constituted, of course, a constant danger to the French presence in these states not only because of common emotional ties among North African Arabs, but because the war has on occasion splashed over the borders of the two states bordering on Algeria. But in spite of the shadow of the Algerian war, Morocco and Tunisia, at least until the Bizerte affair of July 1961, have tended to favor the French presence in its cultural form, and to show toleration toward the French settlers and a respect for their property and financial interests. And even when the battle of Bizerte, which cost the Tunisians at least 1,200 lives, was taking place, foreign observers were impressed by the relative lack of physical molestation to which the *colons* were submitted, and the friendliness between captured Tunisian officers trained at Saint Cyr and their French captors. Whether it was possible, after Bizerte, to still maintain that disputes between Tunisia and France resembled lovers' quarrels, only the future would tell. But this was a comparison foreign observers often made before July 1961. As for Morocco, in spite of Bizerte and the failure of the peace negotiations of Lugrin, King Hassan II, remaining aloof from the plight of his Algerian and Tunisian allies, expressed his deep respect for France and the hope that the friendly relations between Morocco and France would continue.[1]

In the summer of 1960, for example, French officers with their families still strolled about the quiet squares of Bizerte; most of the best farm land in Tunisia was in French hands; Tunis still gave a French impression, especially evenings when newspaper boys hawked the latest issues of *France-Soir*, *Le Monde*, etc., to late afternoon habitués of the innumerable outdoor cafés; and it was not unusual to find a garage owner in the small provincial Tunisian town of Enfida, dressed in slippers, wearing a red skull cap and a cream-colored jallabah serving his customers in fluent French. At the pools of Casablanca often only the darkish complexions of many of the young people swimming would indicate that one was not in a French resort. And a pro-Moroccan Frenchwoman, one of those to sign a petition submitted to the French government recommending negotiations with the Algerian rebels, told of being surprised at how many of the small *colons* of Morocco also signed. She surmised that they had realized independence did not mean exploitation, or sequestration, of their property.

In July 1960, the *Direction Générale des Affaires Culturelles et Techniques* of the French Ministry of Foreign Affairs announced that 500 instructors and 345 French professors were still needed to fill positions for the coming year in both Tunisia and Morocco.[2] In the case of Morocco, these teachers were needed to fulfill the cultural agreement of November 1957, an agreement which assured, according to the Moroccan Foreign Minister, Ahmed Balafrej, permanent contact between the Moroccans "attached to Arab and Islamic culture . . . with the values of French culture whose principal role in the unfolding of human civilization no longer needs to be shown." [3] Morocco and France pledged themselves to encourage the study of the culture of the other in its own country, and France was granted freedom of teaching in its own educational institutions in Morocco which in 1957 served 75,000 French *colon* students. The agreement also provided satisfactory terms for those teachers from France serving the Moroccan government, and private institutions serving 10,000 students were guaranteed their free development. Primary classes were to include three hours of Arabic as a minimum per week in the French schools; these schools were to be open to Moroccan students. The French government also agreed to help the new Moroccan University with the creation of special Chairs.

At the time of the cultural agreement of 1957 the French Cultural Mission was providing education to 9,045 secondary students (2,261 of these, in equal parts, were Moslems and Jews) and to 38,431 primary students (5,337 of whom were Moroccan Moslems and 2,654, Jews).[4] In the Moroccan schools French still occupied a prominent place (10 class hours out of 30 were held in French in the first year, and then 15 in the following years). In secondary education, for want of instructors, the French language was dominant with only thirteen hours out of a total of thirty-three being given in Arabic.[5]

In 1961 the French role in Moroccan education remained as great as ever and in one respect, at least, it had increased. In 1957, 400 Moroccan students had been studying in France; in 1961 the figure had risen to 600.[6] In 1961, also, France was contributing to the advancement of Morocco by providing 8,000 teachers, several hundred doctors, 8,000 functionaries and 1,300 billions (old francs) in private investment.

The French presence from an economic point of view continued to be enormous. France remained the leading export market for Moroccan phosphates and Frenchmen controlled the major part of the modern economy of the country and most of its foreign trade. Figures for 1960 show that most of the top managerial positions in private enterprises were controlled by Frenchmen, and of the 15,000 foreign civil servants working for the state, the bulk were French citizens. The municipal government of Casablanca, Morocco's largest city, had 200 French officials working for it, and one million hectares of the best land in Morocco was in French hands.[7]

In the case of Tunisia, the French authorities were (in 1960) pleased with the manner in which the government was "decolonizing." The cultural relationship of the two countries was governed by the Convention of 1955, which provided guarantees similar to those of the Moroccan convention. In 1960 there were 1,100 teachers of French citizenship in the regular Tunisian school system and the number was expected to increase; in the French system proper, of the 34,322 students, 43 per cent were of Tunisian nationality (8,079 were Moslems, 6,640 were Jews). The remaining were children of members of the European colony which in 1960 stood at around 120,000 persons, 65,000 of whom were French citizens.[8] The new Tunisian system of instruction introduced in 1958 was still heavily French and the University had running through it a French system leading to Sorbonne degrees. In his speech of June 25, 1958, President Bourguiba, in announcing the new system of national education which aimed at increased arabization, recognized that French would be necessary for a long time for want of an Arabic teaching corps.[9]

Before the disaster of Bizerte in July 1961, France financed a great part of the educational system of Tunisia: 45 per cent of the cost of the 1,100 French teachers serving the Tunisian system;

specialized training for 354 officials of the Tunisian government in France; the full cost of the Cultural Mission's 1,500 teachers; and 300 scholarship students in the French university system.

In 1961, the Cultural and University Mission (France's second largest cultural mission abroad) provided education for 32,000 students (of whom 15,000 were Tunisian) in schools manned by 520 teachers (secondary), 182 (technical), and 780 (primary). In Tunisian government schools, there were 274 French teachers in secondary, 111 in technical, and over 1,000 French teachers in primary schools. The higher ranks of the University (*professeurs et maîtres de conférence*) were occupied exclusively by French professors.[10]

The French economic presence before July 1961 was important enough for a Tunisian observer to describe Tunisian economic decolonization as "timid." [11] According to this observer, French landholders produced 40 per cent, in value, of all Tunisian cereals; 10 per cent of olives; and 95 per cent (if some Italians are included) of vintage. The French were also in majority control of Tunisian mining and of the following branches of industry: fertilizers, liquid air, explosives, printing, perfumes, paper, glass, brewing, and metal alloys. Sixty per cent of Tunisia's foreign trade was with France, and the French controlled 72 per cent of Tunisian banking, 50 per cent of freight transport and most of the insurance business. Fifty per cent of taxable income was French. A special trade convention provided Tunisia, in 1960, with benefits including the right to import $76,000,000 of goods duty free into France (the French got preferential treatment for $70,000,000 of their goods). Other benefits, military investments in Bizerte, for example, contributed to a total French investment in Tunisia estimated at $25,000,000 a year. French citizens still controlled 475,000 hectares of land although 43,565 hectares of French-owned land had been expropriated.

Another statistical indication of the French presence in Tunisia was the evidence of a comparison of sales of newspapers and periodicals in the two languages of French and Arabic.[12] Dailies published in France sold 7,778 copies in 1960 (*France-Soir* had the largest circulation with 3,800); Tunisian dailies in French sold 44,000, while the two Arab dailies together sold 30,000. Also sold in Tunisia were 22,173 copies of French magazines of a political nature, 509, economic, 9,805, cultural, and 26,267 women's magazines. Fewer than 500 copies of magazines in English were sold —

the *Reader's Digest* sold 10, and *Time*, 89 (Italian, 7,753 — there are 35,000 Italians who live in Tunisia — and German, 351).[13] The FLN periodical, *El-Moudjahid*, sold 25,000 copies in Tunisia (in either the Arabic or French editions). Most movies in Tunis were dubbed in French and national news shorts were in French five years after independence.

Besides the economic and cultural ties between France and the two North African states, an important part of the French presence has been the physical presence in these states of that part of the *colon* population which chose to remain in North Africa after independence. The number of French citizens living in both Morocco and Tunisia in 1956 was half a million and of these 235,000 had by 1960 returned to metropolitan France. Of those remaining in North Africa in 1960, and the figures are approximate, 200,000 were in Morocco and 65,000 in Tunisia.[14]

The Moroccan *colons* generally shared the racialist attitudes of the Algerian *colons* before independence; with independence many felt abandoned by France, and a mixture of fear and disgust led thousands to leave the country.[15] Those, however, who remained seem to have been treated with remarkable leniency, and five years after independence, they lived in safety and continued their various professions.[16] But fears and prejudices die hard. Jean Lacouture found that the Moroccan *colons* he talked to in September 1959 were surprised at how relatively well they were treated, but they continued to live in a state of anxiety. They heard plans were afoot to sequester and divide old tribal lands and suppress the French press; a law had appeared ordering the dissolution of all foreign associations; and agreements were being discussed involving the eventual withdrawal of all French troops from Morocco.

In Tunisia, on the other hand, before the Bizerte tragedy of July 1961, the atmosphere was more friendly toward the French *colon* than was the case in Morocco. Tunisian politics seemed more rational and consistent than the policies of Morocco, and the Tunisian character softer and more amenable (André Demeerseman speaks of the "douceur" of the Tunisian character). Tunisia's leader, Habib Bourguiba, was considered to be the most tolerant, liberal, and Western-oriented leader in the Arab world.[17] In Tunis, in 1960, the time seemed far off before the jumble of French and Italian would no longer be heard, the large Cathedral, facing the French Embassy on Avenue Bourguiba, would cease to serve Sunday masses to audiences that looked like anything one might see in provincial France, and book stores would stop displaying the latest novels published in Paris.[18] But there were rough edges, the French settler was not completely free from petty annoyances, and typical of the patronizing attitude of the *colons* toward the Tunisians was a remark by a well-educated French woman. "I like the Tunisians," she said, "they are a friendly and gentle people. But of course they are all liars." Generally, the *colons* in the summer of 1960 seemed happier with their lot in independent Tunisia than were their counterparts in Morocco, and their attitude toward the "natives" was less patronizing and less suspicious.

But one year later the situation in Tunisia suddenly changed when Bourguiba decided to put pressure upon the French again to abandon their naval base at Bizerte and cede to Tunisia a part of the Sahara. The French response to Tunisian pressure was as brutal as it was temporarily effective. Whoever was to blame for unleashing the ugly events of July 19–22, observers sympathetic to French-Tunisian cooperation were appalled. Claude Krief, an eyewitness, reported that what shocked the Tunisians the most was the harshness that made the French response to Tunisian demonstrators more of a "lesson" than a defensive action.[19] Jean Daniel concluded that it would take years for the sympathy that had existed between Tunisians and Frenchmen to be revived, and both *L'Express* and *Time* concluded that de Gaulle had "scuttled Bourguibism," that is, the philosophy that maintained decolonization in cooperation with the West was possible.[20] The editor of *Afrique-Action* stated vitriolically that Tunisia had now discovered that cooperation with France could only result in "neo-colonialism" and Mohammed Masmoudi, the most pre-French of the Tunisian leaders according to Jean Lacouture, condemned France and gave high praise to Nasser as having been right all along in dealing militantly with the West.[21]

What the long-run consequences of the Bizerte affair would be it was impossible to say, but by September 1961, it appeared that even though several thousand French citizens had emigrated to France,[22] the hostilities aroused by the affair seemed to have subsided. Tunisia and France were able to negotiate the Bizerte question and diplomatic and cultural relations were renewed.[23] But many Tunisians now believed that full sovereignty might be incompatible with close cultural and economic ties to France.

This is what Cairo had been preaching to the Tunisians over the Voice of Arabs. And this appeared to be the point of view of the Moroccan leftists [24] and of the new president of the Algerian Provisional Government (GPRA) who replaced Ferhat Abbas in August 1961.[25] With incidents like that of Bizerte, and with the prolongation of the Algerian war which affected all North Africans whether Algerian or not, France, and so the West, seemed to be paying a high price for the ideal of French grandeur.

IV

ALGERIAN *COLONS* AND THE CRISIS OF THE FRENCH PRESENCE

The relationship that has prevailed between France and Morocco and Tunisia since independence in 1956 will not necessarily prove to be a model for France's relationship to independent Algeria. Algeria was an integral part of metropolitan France, while her two sister states were only protectorates and never lost their complete political identity. Algeria has also been under French rule for many more years than the other two states, and her economic and political life has been dominated by a much larger *colon* population than has been the case with Tunisia and Morocco. Another difference between the experience of these states is that the Tunisians and Moroccans obtained their independence with relative ease and without the enormous sacrifice of eight years of revolution that the Algerians have endured. As an ironic result of the difference in the experience of the three peoples, the French presence might prove to be most vulnerable, one day, in that part of North Africa in which it has been the most deeply rooted, culturally and materially.

In 1961 it was impossible to predict the future of the French presence in Algeria. However, it could be said that a crucial factor in determining this future was the behavior of the large French minority [1] which at that time still dominated the political and economic life of the country.[2] This Algerian *colon* bloc has had a notorious reputation among students of the North African scene. It has been called racialist, and it has been considered to be the main barrier to needed reforms in Algeria. It is blamed by many young Moslem *évolués* for the disillusionment with the possibility of assimilation. And until quite recently, it has been treated as the tail that wags the dog in French politics. Julien has described the *colons* as "biologically opposed to reform"; General Catroux found them to be "congenitally minors"; Jules Ferry, the nineteenth century French imperialistic statesman, once wrote:

"It is difficult to make the European *colon* understand that there are other rights than his in an Arab land. . . . ," [3] and Germaine Tillion reports: "One day in 1955 a workman in Algiers said, without the slightest irony: 'First of all, everyone to his own country. The Arabs to Arabia. . . .' " [4]

As early as 1841 Alexis de Tocqueville, on a parliamentary mission to Algeria, wrote prophetically of the atmosphere of the small frontier settlements he visited. A colonel in Philippeville said of the Arabs, "Only force and terror, my dear sirs, work with those fellows," and he boasted of having decapitated an Arab on the basis of pure suspicion of murder and placed his head over the gateway of Constantine. He then spoke disparagingly of the French settlers as "canailles" only interested in using the army to promote their own ends. A sailor in the audience took exception to this, arguing that only by dispossessing the Arabs and settling Frenchmen could France consolidate her position in Algeria. "And I," wrote Tocqueville, "listening to these things with sadness, asked myself what the future of the country in the hands of men such as these could possibly be, and how this cascade of violence and injustice could end but in the revolt of the native and the ruin of the Europeans?" [5] Had much changed by 1913? In this year a book by a *colon*, André Servier, entitled *Le nationalisme musulman*, was published and went through three editions among a people that, C.-A. Julien states, reads very little.[6] The Moslems are presented as incapable of any loyalty, responsive only to force, and as belonging to an inferior race. Recent studies of the *colon* population of Algeria, the two books by Jules Roy and by Pierre Nora, for example, indicate that the attitude of the bulk of the *colons* toward the Moslem Arabs had not changed in the post-World War II period.[7]

Perhaps the saddest consequence of the racialism of the *colons* has been its influence upon French-educated Algerians who once genuinely loved France and tried to identify themselves with the French nation. Such a person was the young Ferhat Abbas, in later years to join the rebellion against a France which had allowed the *colons* to betray the hopes of himself and of his colleagues. "France," he stated in the twenties, "created military service for the natives to encourage them to participate in the life of the nation: the Colony was hostile to this measure. France gave us the law of February 4, 1919 [which provided for some representation of Moslems in local government]: the Colony was hostile to this law. France envisions the possibility of native representation in Parliament: the Colony is hostile to such representation. France organized aid to women in delivery: the Colony was hostile to this assistance. France opened its land to the Algerian worker: the Colony is hostile to the exodus of the Algerian worker to France. . . ." He quoted the ironic statement made by Anatole France in *Sur la pierre blanche*: "France for seventy years despoiled, hunted down, ferreted out the Arabs to populate Algeria with Italians and Spaniards!" And Abbas warned the followers of the *colon* propagandist, Louis Bertrand, who wanted a "Roman" Algeria dominated to perpetuity by the European minority: ". . . in reality, the 'Bastion' of M. Louis Bertrand bears an exact resemblance to those marvellous castles raised upon the back of a sleeping animal. The monster moves, the castle comes crashing down, and all vanishes." [8]

It would be wrong, however, to think of the *colon* bloc as completely monolithic, as possessing only one predictable point of view toward the Moslems and their problems. There have been liberal *colons* of the ilk of Chevallier, the liberal mayor of the city of Algiers, Pierre Popie, and writers like Albert Camus, Jules Roy, Jean Daniel, and Jean Pelegri.[9] But theirs has been a minority attitude, and an attitude that was not particularly effective judging by the Algerian situation in 1961. Also, the liberal *colons* were subject to enormous pressure and even terrorism, as Thomas Brady reported as early as 1957, and the "ultra" point of view has always been able to dominate the strategic capital of Algiers.[10] It is here that the political pace was set most dramatically in May 1958 when the Fourth Republic was destroyed in large part on the steps of the Forum.

By the summer of 1960 it seemed evident to an outside observer that since the accession of General de Gaulle to power in 1958 the tide had turned against the *colons*. But it was also apparent that the bulk of the *colon* population, however disillusioned it might have become with de Gaulle and with the prospects for their future in Algeria, were determined to oppose and to obstruct this tide of the future by all means at their disposal. In effect, this meant that any attempted resolution of the Algerian problem would most probably be marked with racial violence. This proved to be the case by the following year. By the summer of 1961 one felt that with the explosion of every plastic bomb and with every lynching, the *colon* population was destroying any possible future it might have in an independent Algeria. It was difficult any longer to believe that judging by the toleration of French settlers in Morocco and Tunisia, a *modus vivendi* could be worked out in Algeria. It was no longer possible to feel confident that the horrors of the Congo might not be repeated in Algeria. As an astute observer of the Algerian scene pointed out in October 1961, de Gaulle may have lost any chance of a humane and equitable peace by not having negotiated this peace by the autumn of 1960 at the latest.[11] A year later the Secret Army Organization had come into existence, and racial violence was the order of the day.

The extent to which the situation in Algeria had disintegrated between 1960 and 1961 is illustrated by a brief interview the author had with the mayor of G . . . , a municipality on the outskirts of Algiers. This mayor was a liberal and a supporter of de Gaulle, and the observations that he made seemed reasonable and plausible to the author at the time. According to the mayor, the situation in Algeria had improved since May 1958 when many *colons* began to claim that most Moslems of Algeria were really supporters of "Algérie Française" and would, in the future, be treated like brothers. This was the newly discovered myth of "integration." At first, "integration" for most *colons* was a case of pretence or self-delusion, but, gradually, the mayor believed, the *colons* were coming to accept this myth as reality and to reconcile themselves to Moslem equality. "When you go to Tunis," he told the author, "tell Ferhat Abbas if you should meet him what I have said. We used to be good friends. I would like him to know that things have changed for the better since he lost faith and joined the rebels. . . ." According to the mayor, 10 per cent of the Arabs were completely on the side of the rebel National Liberation Front, a somewhat smaller number with the French, and all the others were simply waiting on the sidelines. He approved of de Gaulle's policy of offering self-determination to the Algerians (in September 1959), and he hoped ultimately for federation of the Maghreb attached to France. He deplored the racialism among the *colons*, which he admitted still existed, but he also felt that without intimidation 40 to 50 per cent of the French in Algeria would vote for a liberal Gaullist policy. One year later, in 1961, the assessments and hopes of the liberal mayor of G . . . . had become tragically obsolete. By this time it appeared that the ideal of integration had suffered a mortal blow as had the confidence *colons* like the mayor once had had in de Gaulle's policies. And it seemed evident that if the majority of Moslem Arabs had simply been waiting in 1960 to see which way the wind would blow, they had made their decision by 1961, and their decision was for an independent Algeria under the control of the FLN. Mendès-France could say with little fear of contradiction in metropolitan France in September 1961: "Everyone now knows that Algeria will be independent. Everyone knows that Algeria will be governed by the FLN. . . ." [12]

It was also revealing of the distintegration of the Algerian situation by 1961 to compare the racial violence and brutality in Oran in the summer of this year with the Oran of 1960 when the French and the Arabs, though not warmly disposed toward each other, seemed to be able to cooperate in their daily activities. Oran in 1960 was the most tranquil of all the Algerian cities. But there were warning signals — the growing loss of hope among the French settlers, a disillusionment which was to be transformed into the violence and hysteria of a year later.[13] In 1960 the *colons* began to lose heart after the events of January when de Gaulle had suppressed the revolt of Algiers and had arrested both Lagaillarde, the popular hero of the "ultras," and the powerful and influential editor of the *Echo d'Alger*, Alain de Sérigny. The *colons* had already turned against de Gaulle when he had offered self-determination to the Algerians, but it was in January they had learned that they could not count on the French army to support their cause for the time being at least. The Oranese had begun to wonder how long they would be able to proclaim "Ici la France" in large painted letters at the entrance of their harbor. The feeling of growing defeatism appeared in conversations with *colons*. A patron of a small bar, who once worked on a large domain as a farm hand, was convinced the FLN had by no means been beaten, that it would not be, that only the army was keeping it suppressed. A *colon* taxi driver, who spoke Spanish as well as French, but not a word of Arabic, blamed the revolution on the fact that the Arabs had never been "really civilized." Typically, he believed that even a rich Arab who buys a bed prefers to sleep on the floor, and that any Arab girl without a veil must surely be a prostitute. But the peacefulness of the city, he maintained, proved that the Arabs and French of Oran had no difficulty in living together. He would live under a tolerant Arab government in principle, but he was sure that under the Arabs, the *colons* would, in fact, be crushed. The idea, however, of taking his family to France was unreal to him. "This is my home, I don't know anything about France," he said. An elderly hotel clerk told that he had taken his present job after resigning as a gendarme. His health had broken down after terrorists had wounded him twice, once while he was on guard at an open-air movie house into which a grenade had been thrown. "Our heroes," he said, "are Massu and Juin. Ever since he uttered the phrase 'Algerian Algeria,' de Gaulle couldn't get more than 10 per cent of the French Algerian vote in an election. The rebels are savages, like the Congolese. By pussy-footing with them we are losing Algeria. We need a Massu, not a de Gaulle."

This impression of disillusionment was confirmed by a letter which Jean Cohen, a teacher in Oran, wrote to *Le Monde* in July 1960 entitled "La grand peur des 'petits blancs'." Today, the author stated, the small *colon* is no longer aggressively self-confident, but on the defensive. He is inspired by fear that the Algeria of tomorrow will be the exact opposite of what he has known. It will be an Algeria in which the roles of superior and inferior would be reversed. "Be logical," an Oranese said to Cohen, "if you have some trouble with an 'Arab' do you expect that an Arab policeman is likely to defend you?" Racialists in their mentality, they were incapable of seeing any situation but their own in reverse; they knew nothing about the Arabs, they were plagued by fantastic fears which, Cohen believed, the FLN should do more to allay.

What was the attitude of the FLN towards the French Algerians? Were the anxieties of the *colons* justified as to what independence would mean for them? There was no way of answering these questions for certain, but it could be assumed that the longer and the more difficult the war, the less indulgent and tolerant Arab nationalists would be likely to be. Officially, and in all of their declarations of policy, the FLN had declared that the French Algerians would be offered every opportunity to live as citizens of Algeria or to leave the country if they so preferred; they would simply cease to be a dominant and privileged minority.[14] And in his *L'an V de la révolution algérienne*, Frantz Fanon, who worked with the Army of National Liberation (ALN) in Algeria, took considerable pains to try to prove that the European minority was not monolithic, and that members of it have collaborated with the FLN or at least sympathized with it. Among such Europeans were French farmers who have stocked ALN food supplies, and even, on occasion, handed over weapons to soldiers of the ALN. Some French doctors and pharmacists also have ignored orders and administered medical aid to wounded rebel Arab soldiers. Fanon published some letters from French Algerians supporting the FLN. One example is that of a young man named Bresson Yvon, born in Bône (Algeria), who confessed to having collaborated closely with the FLN in various ways: "It was as an Algerian," he wrote, "that I did these things. I had no impression of having betrayed France. I am an Algerian and like every Algerian I fought and continue to fight colonialism. As a conscientious Algerian citizen, my place was by the side of the patriots. . . ." [15] How significant for the future this collaboration between the Algerian rebels and a few French will be only the future can tell. But one would think that in transcending their racialist upbringing, these young French Algerians were making at least a symbolically important contribution to a future when the Algerian Frenchman and Moslem might be able to realize a common *modus vivendi*.[16]

But of course the few Frenchmen who have decided to identify themselves with the Algerian rebels constitute a small and unrepresentative minority. More important in influencing the future of relations between the French settlers and the Moslems would have been moral and intellectual leaders among the *colons*, able to transcend their narrow provincialism and prove to the Moslems that a Frenchman could genuinely respect their right to equality and dignity. The outstanding *colon* who might have taken such a lead was Albert Camus.

Jules Roy has said of Camus: "He was the first to draw the attention of his compatriots (the Algerian *colons*) to the misery of the Kabyle (the Berber region in northern Algeria) and to demand justice for the Algerian people in 1939. . . . If Camus had not written, many of us would have wandered aimlessly across the fatality of our existence." [17] And for the nationalistic writers of the North African literary movement of the fifties, Camus was an important stimulus and inspiration — to them Camus was something of a culture-hero. But by the time of his death in 1960, Camus had failed to win the confidence of the *colons* and had lost the confidence of the Moslem nationalists. He was the victim of the ironic and even tragic dilemma into which history has forced many French *colons*, and French *colons* at their most generous. The story of Camus' failure is not a happy one, but it is significant in the context of this study and deserves to be told.

The setting of Camus' writing was usually North Africa — Algiers (*L'étranger*) and Oran (*La peste*) — and the North African sun illumines his work and serves as something of a symbol of grace in his philosophy. How, he asked in his first book, could youths brought up in North Africa, however poor and miserable they might be, deny the possibility of happiness as a dimension of life when their bones were always warmed by the Mediterranean sun? Above all, a spirit of moral revolt inspires his books, a spirit akin to that of many contemporary young Moslems. It is understandable, therefore, that an important book like *As-Sud*,[18] a modern Tunisian poetic drama by Messadi, should reflect the theme of *Le mythe de Sisyphe*; that a Moroccan intellectual could say that many of his generation had learned to see themselves honestly for the first time after reading *L'étranger*; and that the favorite contemporary work for a young Tunisian schoolteacher was the play, *Les justes*.

Camus, born at Mondovi in the Constantine in 1913 of a French farm laborer and a mother of Spanish origin, was educated in Algeria at the University of Algiers, and even after moving to France to fight in the Resistance and then to remain there, he continued, in his Nobel Prize speech, for example, to refer to himself as an Algerian. He encouraged members of the new school of North African writers, many of them Moslems,[19] by writing prefaces to some of their works, and he saw in this artistic community a bridge between France and Moslem Algeria which might outlast the Algerian war. In an interview in November 1957, he declared: ". . . I would like to recall that there was once a community of Algerian writers, French and Arab. For the moment this community is cut in two. But men such as Feraoun, Mammeri, Chraibi, Dib, and so many others have taken their place among European writers. No matter what the future may be, no matter how hopeless it may look, I am sure that this will not be forgotten." [20]

Camus participated, for a period, in the Algerian debate and bore indignant witness to the inadequacies of much of French administrative policy in articles in *Alger Républicain* and elsewhere (collected as *Actuelles*, vol. III). But he participated as a Frenchman, because to him Algeria was as much France as it is to any proponent of integration today. His attack on French maladministration was sweeping and uncompromising. He accused the government of distributing food (in near-famine times in the Kabyle) unequally to Arabs and French, and of failing to distribute enough (1945). He declared: "Don't they realize that in this country where the sky and the earth invite one to happiness, millions are suffering from hunger?" He blamed the French government for the disillusionment of those Moslems who had once hoped to become French citizens and he attacked it for succumbing to the influence of the "grands colons." It was too late, he insisted, for de Gaulle to solve anything by offering citizenship to 80,000 after the war, when in 1936 France had allowed the *colons* to defeat a bill which would have given citizenship to 60,000. He criticized the French in Algeria for being unaware of the fact that the Moslems were no longer an "amorphous mass" but had reached a state of proud self-consciousness. In 1956 he denounced the government for giving in to *colon* pressures and allowing the *colons* to determine national policy during a period of socialist government. He deplored the pitifulness of the government's educational efforts in Algeria, and he ridiculed the policy of limiting citizenship, in the case of Berbers, to those who agreed to abandon their Moslem status. He wrote: "It is we ourselves who have imposed this status on the Kabyles in arabizing their country with the caidat (Moslem administration) and with the introduction of Arabic. And we hardly have the right today to reproach the Kabyles for something we ourselves have imposed upon them."

But when what seemed like a revolt in 1954 turned into the Algerian revolution, and after a brief but futile attempt to persuade both sides to repudiate terroristic tactics, Camus refused to comment any further on the war or to take sides. This position was consistent with the logic of his politico-moralistic essay, *L'homme révolté*, as well as of his play, *Les justes*. In both, he repudiated "revolution" whose tactics inevitably lead to the illegitimate repudiation of human value and sanctity and so lead to nihilism. He contrasted "revolution" with "revolt" which legitimately and honorably seeks to combat evil but which is conducted with a love for the persons of the enemy and a sense of limitation (the awareness that evil can never be totally eliminated). Camus' aloofness was thus inspired by moral conviction as well as by his dual loyalty to France and Algeria.[21]

The only solution that he had offered to the Algerian question, before his self-chosen isolation, was that of a federation of the

Algerian peoples to be closely associated with France. Such a solution should be imposed, he said, and not negotiated with the FLN. Negotiation, he was convinced, would lead to the recognition of Algerian independence, place Algeria in the hands of implacable militants and terrorists, humiliate France, and lead to the eviction of the European. The alternative to his solution he felt, would be to allow the growth of "an Islamic empire" which could only multiply the misery of the masses. There had never been an Algerian nation, he declared, and Jews and Berbers were as indigenous as the Arabs. Arab nationalism meant for him control by Egypt's Nasser and ultimately by the U.S.S.R.

To the militants of Algeria, naturally, and to Moroccans and Tunisians, Camus' attitude was an obvious disappointment, almost a betrayal. The Algerian poet Yacine spoke for many when he said of Camus: "At one time he was the friend of the people. This was understandable during the period of paternalism when the power of the popular front had not yet come into being. But this popular front is now present and he is afraid; he hides himself behind attitudes such as: if I had to choose between justice and my mother, I would pick my mother . . . ," [22] and Yacine also dismissed the pernicious "exoticism" of *L'étranger* and other works in which Camus "weds himself to Algeria only on the surface." A young member of the FLN in Tunis, an intellectual of French origin born in Algiers (and so, as he put it, "one of a minority of a minority" in having joined the FLN) dismisses Camus as of insignificant influence among the Arabs. As he expressed it, Camus "is an unrealistic moralist, a preacher of a type of fraternalism which is disguised paternalism. Arabs in his books are only part of the back-drop. He is a Frenchman who only happened to have been born in Algeria. . . ."

A less partisan and more generous estimate of Camus in the context of North Africa appears in an article, "Camus parmi nous," by a Moroccan intellectual, Negib Bouderbala. This article was written after Camus' death in 1960.[23] Bouderbala pays tribute to the great influence of *L'étranger* which, he writes, "with one blow, forced us to be born into metaphysical consciousness." It made young Moroccans aware of themselves as strangers, caught passively between two cultures, the French and the Moslem, and of their "solitude." [24] In contrast to his deliberate engagement in the struggle against Nazism, however, Camus disappointed his admirers when the Algerian question reached the stage of revolution: "For many of us who expected this voice to defend our justice as the only justice, this was a sort of resignation. . . . We — Algerians, Moroccans, Tunisians — saw this retreat as a great weakness. Camus had abandoned a human fraternity; he left others to fight placing his own precious innocence in an ivory tower; he washed his hands of us." Camus' remark in Stockholm about choosing his mother rather than justice, though a sort of verbal sally, seemed to young North Africans to show a lack of courage; but nevertheless, the writer ends: "This man is dead and we loved him, why not admit it?"

Camus' reputation as a writer on an international plane remains, but as a voice and a conscience in the Algerian revolt, as Raymond Aron puts it, "in spite of his desire for justice, his generosity, M. Albert Camus fails to rise above the attitude of the colonizer of good will." [25] Albert Memmi suggests in his *Portrait d'un colonisé* that the colonizer of good will is placed in "an impossible historical situation," impossible because a colonial revolution inevitably produces a xenophobic spirit and a re-emergence of at least lip service to traditional religious ideas. Oftentimes, also, because of the relative weakness of the revolutionaries, terrorism is used as a tactic.[26] These characteristics of the revolution shock the sense of values of the liberal and make it difficult for him to identify himself with a cause whose future promises to be so different from the future he might desire.[27] As a universal proposition this may be an overstatement — but Memmi's comment is relevant, sadly, to the case of Albert Camus as French Algerian — at least relevant for many he once knew as friends and allies.

But although disappointed with the stand of a *colon* of such influence and generosity as Camus, the Algerian rebel did find support and comfort in moralists and intellectuals in metropolitan France. Members of the Catholic Church, for example, realized the tragic cost of attempting to maintain an unwanted presence in North Africa. They saw contemporary colonialism as a danger to the Christian presence. Thus the White Fathers, who originally supported French imperialism, were neutral following the Second World War, and even sympathetic to the nationalists in the opinion of many *colons*. And Catholic writers like Robert de Montavalon and Robert Barrat openly defended the cause of Algerian, as well as Moroccan and Tunisian, independence.[28] Intellectuals like Raymond Aron, author of the influential *The Algerian Tragedy*, argued that it is irrational from an economic point of view to maintain that Algeria could remain French, and in the summer of 1960 the leaders of the National Union of Students of France (UNEF) joined with their Algerian counterpart, the Moslem Algerian Students' Union (UGEMA), to issue a statement demanding immediate negotiations with the FLN. The most dramatic protest against the Algerian war came from the pen of Francis Jeanson and his colleagues in the form of the so-called "petition of the 121." A wide variety of French intellectuals and artists put their names to this document which contained, among other radical propositions, the following statement: "We respect and consider justified the refusal to take up arms against the Algerian people — we respect and consider justified the conduct of Frenchmen who hold it their duty to give aid and protection to the oppressed Algerians in the name of the French people. The cause of the Algerian people, contributing in a decisive fashion to the ruin of the colonial system, is the cause of all free men." [29]

This position adopted by some French liberals had more than a rhetorical significance. Luethy said that the French, whose clocks do not keep the same time as clocks of others, can exhibit the worst type of provincialism. But these intellectuals at least testified to the fact that Frenchmen could also stand courageous witness against this very provincialism. There are grounds for the ambivalence of many French-educated North African *évolués* toward a France they can respect and perhaps love again. The rebels have little confidence in the *colons* — they have seen that even someone like Albert Camus failed them — but they might be prepared some day to renew the cultural dialogue with the intellectuals of metropolitan France who have appreciated and even defended the values of the Algerian revolution.

V

"CULTURAL OPPRESSION" AND THE
REJECTION OF ASSIMILATION

By the end of the Second World War, many North African nationalists still respected and loved French culture often more than their own cultural heritage. But they had repudiated the ideal of cultural assimilation to France. They might be unable to read or to speak in Arabic, but they had decided that their children should be raised in the language and culture of Islam, and they condemned France for her policy of what Paul Sebag has called "oppression culturelle." [1]

Two of the most thoughtful attacks upon the ideal of assimilation appear in the books (both written in French) by the Tunisian Albert Memmi and the Algerian Malek Bennabi. [2] Both authors insisted that the policy of cultural assimilation could only produce cultural misfits, men without any cultural roots or any genuine values. They maintained that this policy had been used to divorce elites from contact with the mass of their compatriots, and they argued that the *évolué* could only find his identity in rediscovering his roots in the traditional culture that French colonialists had disparaged and repressed. On a more popular level, this condemnation of the policy of assimilation is expressed in a brochure issued by the FLN: [3]

Colonialism has attacked the cultural and religious heritage of the Algerian nation, intent on depersonalizing the masses so as to exploit them further and to implement the policy of "assimilation." The national language of the Algerian people is Arabic. Colonialism has sought to stamp out the Arabic language. The results of this policy are characterized at present by the refusal to allow the teaching of Arabic in government schools and by many hindrances to free education. Only in the Higher Institute of Islamic Studies, and three Medersas (secondary schools), attended by less than five hundred students, are Arabic studies pursued. In the French secondary schools, Arabic is taught as a foreign language. The establishment of free primary schools is openly hampered by the authorities who frequently close them down and arrest the teachers. A teacher (Cheickh Zerrouki) has been condemned to four years' imprisonment for teaching Algerian history. Even education in French is very limited. The percentage of illiteracy is ninety per cent and today two million school-age children are deprived of any education. . . . French education in Algeria aims at depersonalizing the Algerians who are taught "your ancestors were the Gauls."

A more personal but equally intense attack upon French cultural policies was made in a speech delivered in Beirut on June 16, 1961, by Malek Haddad.[4] He described the Algerian situation as "the most perfidious case of depersonalization in history," a case of "cultural asphyxia," and he cited his own inability to address his audience in Arabic as an illustration of France's success in suppressing the Algerian's personality — "the French language is my exile," he stated. He referred to his own generation of poets and novelists as an anachronism and insisted that only successful "neo-colonialism" could allow French to remain the medium of creative expression in an independent Algeria.

Part of the accusation of the évolués of Morocco against the French on the cultural level has been the French attempt to encourage separatist Berber cultural development; to allow Maraboutism (superstitious saint-worship) to flourish while discouraging the reformist Islamic movement; and to force the Christian presence on a Moslem people.[5] However, religious problems, important as they are, are not in the province of this monograph, which is concerned primarily with the question of education.

The French answer to the accusations of the nationalists was, first, that the same statistics the nationalists cited could be used to show how much France did do, considering the enormous obstacles presented, and to point to the high standards — those of France proper — they maintained in their schools; and second, that the French had recognized in recent years the need to teach and educate in Arabic as well as in French, and had moved in this direction. The French were confronted with a total absence of any modern institutions when they first arrived in North Africa (the primitive koranic schools and the medievalist universities like Qarawiyin represented an ossified culture unsuitable for modern life). The French were obliged to preserve order in rebellious regions and in very difficult terrain. And the "population explosion," a result of France's success in eliminating epidemics, precluded the possibility of offering Moslems modern education either rapidly or comprehensively.

In spite of all these difficulties, some French have argued, an enormous amount was accomplished. In Morocco in 1944 there were 32,270 students in school; 16,171 were in primary schools, 1,397 in *écoles de notables*, 854 in the first classes of high schools, 5,498 in apprentice schools, 568 in secondary classes, and 7,582 girls were being trained in European-style handicraft. In 1943, only thirty-one years after the protectorate had been established, there were 146 Moroccan *bacheliers* and 20 *licenciés*.[6]

But the Moroccan nationalist will cite other facts and figures. In 1955 there were one million and a half children of school age in Morocco. Of these only 287,000 were in school. Private efforts by nationalists like Ahmed Balafrej, encouraged by the Sultan, to provide education in Arabic were at best ignored by the French authorities.[7] All secondary education was in French, and even in the French-Moslem primary schools — designed to educate partly in Arabic — twenty out of thirty hours were in French, and no provision was made for the study of Arabic-Islamic culture.[8] In addition, Arab nationalists have argued, there is evidence since independence that the French failed to promote attendance as rapidly as they might have done. An official in the Moroccan Ministry of Education said to the author (in 1960): ". . . the proof of this is that under the French something less than 100,000 students were enrolled in school (in Morocco) while now we have 700,000 students in primary schools alone. Forty years of French rule might have been useful in part, but it lasted too long. In four years we have done what the French would not have done in twenty. We have had the sense of urgency and dedication the French never had, Morocco is our country."

In the case of Tunisia the French defended their educational system before the United Nations with the following facts and statistics: until 1845 the only source of education was Zaitouna, the Islamic university, and *kuttabs*, small koranic schools, presided over by graduates of the former; emphasis was on reading, writing, and recitation of the Koran.[9] No girls at all received instruction. In 1875–76 the progressive minister, Khayr ad-Din, opened the famous Collége Sadiqi which gave education in both Arabic and French. The French supported this school after their occupation of Tunisia in 1881. The plan for 1949–69 aimed at increasing enrollment and offering the Tunisian elite what they wanted, that is, a comprehensive government education combining French and Arabic education.[10] In 1954, 304,530 students were in school, (8.2 per cent of the population), in contrast to 1947

when 182,525 (5.5 per cent of the population) were in school.[11]
The French supervised education in two types of schools, French
and French-Arab (in which by 1954 science was being taught in
Arabic), and there were modern private koranic schools which
were privately financed. Two institutions gave higher degrees,
the *Institut des Hautes Etudes* in Law and the *Direction des Anti-
quités* in Tunisian archeology. French schools taught, in 1954,
59,281 students on a primary level (of these 14,525 were Moslems, the rest French, Italians and Jews). At the same time, on a
primary level, the French-Arab schools taught 125,859 students,
of whom 764 students were not Moslems. In secondary school,
divided into the three sections of *classique, moderne, tunisien*,
15,574 students were accommodated (5,988 were French and only
7,346 were Moslem). In higher education, 668 students were
French and 635 were Moslems out of a total of 1,542. Those who
received their *baccalauréat*, first part, in 1954 numbered 455 (168
French and 211 Moslems, 68 Jews and 8 others); those who received their *baccalauréat*, second part, 317; (165 French, 98 Moslems, 48 Jews and 6 others). Sadiqi, which was wholly Moslem,
graduated 78 students in 1954. The plan of September 22, 1949,
proposed an increase in the number of hours of Arabic to be
used in the French-Arab schools. The result would have been:
11:20 hours of Arabic and 17 hours of French in urban boys'
schools, and 9:50 Arabic and 18:30 French in rural schools and
in girls' schools. Thus, even according to this more progressive
plan, French would still have been the predominant language in
these French-Arab schools.

In his *Tunisie nouvelle: problèmes et perspectives*, Salah-Eddine
Tlatli gives a Tunisian nationalist interpretation of education under the French.[12] Before the French arrived, Tunisia was by no
means an educational desert: education was provided gratis in
primary and secondary schools to 800 students, Zaitouna was a
flourishing university serving all North Africa, and twelve graduates of Sadiqi were on scholarship in France. The French, upon
their arrival, discouraged Arabic education, ignored the koranic
schools, and only permitted the model French-Arab primary
school, the Khaldunia, to open after great pressure.[13] Sadiqi itself
was tampered with and Frenchmen were appointed to teach
Arabic and Arab history — the second they taught, Tlatli states,
in caricature form.[14] In 1920 there were only 10,690 Moslem students in school,[15] of a school population of four times this num-

ber, and Tlatli testified to the personal experience of having been discouraged by the Resident himself from going to France to pursue higher studies.

By 1956 Morocco and Tunisia were able to forge their own way and reverse the educational process, beneficent or not, once imposed upon them. For these two countries the problem of reviving and renovating the traditional Arabic culture was easier than it would be for Algeria. They had been ruled by France for shorter periods and as protectorates only. In addition, the institutions of traditional culture (the universities of Zaitouna and Qarawiyin, for example) might have become sterile but they were still extant and continued throughout the period of the protectorate to disseminate and defend the Arabic language and culture. Conversely, the elites of Tunisia and Morocco, who received a modern education, were also in a much better position to learn literary Arabic (at Sadiqi, for example) than were their fellow-Moslems in Algeria. In addition, Algerian nationalists observe, the French, principally because of the influence of the *colons*, permitted only a small number of Algerians to receive any education at all. The divorce between the elite and the masses in Algeria has been, as a result, much more acute than in the rest of the French-speaking Maghreb.

In Algeria, in 1944, an official French bulletin states there were 110,000 Moslems in school, and in 1954–55 there were 320,000.[16] But in secondary education, out of 40,000 students only 7,500 were Moslem; the University of Algiers had about 500 Moslem students out of about 5,000.[17] Vocational and technical education in 1954–55 was provided to 6,000 Moslems. In 1957 all *colon* children went to school in Algeria; 19 out of 100 Moslems went to school, and there were 317,000 Moslems in government schools in October, one-eighth of the total school age population. In 1954 one girl in sixteen received education, and only 6 per cent of the men and 2 per cent of the women are literate in French. Private efforts, principally by the reformist Ulema (Moslem elders), eager to counter the Catholic French influence among the Moslem young, led to the establishment of schools, most of them primary, that in 1960 served about 150,000 students. The French government granted them at best an uneasy tolerance. In government schools, until 1947, only two hours of Arabic were taught and this was optional; increases after this year were minimal.[18]

During the revolutionary war, the number of Moslems being

educated in the French language increased rather than decreased. In 1954 the number of Moslem students at the University of Algiers was 589 and in 1960 it was 814, and 1,250 Moslems were pursuing higher studies in metropolitan France.[19] Others were studying, for obvious political reasons, in many other parts of the world, but many of those were students in Belgium, Switzerland and Canada where their studies were also conducted in French. It is significant that at the Fourth Congress (in July 1960) of the Moslem Algerian Students' Union, members of the elite of tomorrow's Algeria conducted its deliberations exclusively in French.[20] In 1957 the leadership of the FLN included, besides Abbas, who is completely French educated, Mohammed Lamine-Debbaghine, a French-trained doctor, Mahmoud Cherif, a graduate of a French officers school, Belkacem Krim, who had nine years of French primary education and was a corporal in the French army, Amar Ouamrane, who had six years of French primary education, and Ramdane Abbane who completed his *baccalauréat* in a French *lycée* in Algeria. Unusual in his education was Abdelhamid Mehri who graduated from the traditionalist Islamic university of Zaitouna in Tunis.[21] And the chief representative of the GPRA at the Melun Conference in 1960 was Ahmed Boumendjel, a French-educated lawyer, whose wife still lived in Paris where his two daughters were studying in a Paris *lycée*.

Very helpful in understanding the educational experience of many of the leaders of the Algerian rebel movement is an article by Dr. Sadek Hadjeres, a leftist Algerian political leader and intellectual.[22] The theme of the article is the adventure of young Algerian Moslems educated in French schools and the protagonist is the author himself. The paragraphs that follow are, essentially, a summary of this article.

It was in 1888 that the French first decided, because of their need of administrative auxiliaries, to enforce obligatory schooling among the Moslems. The effort was meagre and restricted, since ten years later, according to a French authority (the university rector, Jeanmaire), 97 per cent of the Moslem children of Algeria remained "strangers to the French language and to all aspects of civilization." (Even on the eve of World War II, Moslem Algerian students totalled only 10 per cent.) Hadjeres was one of the privileged, coming from a Berber family that had enjoyed French education for two generations, and he went to a French school. However, because of the piety of his mother, he also attended, when time allowed, a koranic school run according to old-fashioned methods (chanting, memorizing, etc.). The boy resented this seemingly unimportant and regressive extra-curricular responsibility and was happy to see the French authorities close the school down. But to appease his mother, he continued to study Arabic in his French school as an elective. In later years he was to look back on the elementary Arabic education he had received with gratitude; it had provided something, however primitive, to save him from being wholly cut off from his people and from Islamic culture. He recalls, for example, that he and his friends were not overwhelmed with the grandeur of Durandel, Roland's sword, because the sheikh had described to them the sabre with which Sidna Ali had felled scores of unbelievers. At the French school he and his companions were "civilized" in various ways: mockery of their *sheshias* (headgear: "red cheeses") led to sartorial changes; the use of attractive modern textbooks; the alternating of manual work and gymnastics with their regular study; and the opening of new horizons attracted them to French culture. The education they received was definitely "assimilationist."

The subject that most confused him and his friends was history. Images of Druids cutting mistletoe, of the heroic postures of Joan of Arc and so forth, made them wonder who their own ancestors were, and whether it was true that they had only entered history "to offer themselves to the club of Charles Martel"; to capture the good Saint Louis; to be conquered as cheats and fanatics; and to be given education and assistance in spite of their treacherous and ungrateful revolt in 1871. The picture presented to them was so extreme that they tended to rejected it totally. Hadjeres recalls that at home his maternal grandmother still wept when she told of the seizure of her father's land by Alsace-Lorrainers in 1871.

But the absurdities of history in primary school gave way in secondary school (for the few who reached it) to a maturer picture of the world; different cultures were studied; common themes in different cultures including the Islamic were suggested; and it was made evident that culture had existed in other forms than the French. Also, though the teaching was poor and taken lightly by teachers and students alike (they were taught endless comic folk tales), Arabic could be studied as a second language. Hadjeres was particularly fortunate to have as a teacher an Algerian who took Arabic culture and language seriously and who forced the students to work hard and to read serious texts of Arabic literature. But this teacher was exceptional.

Secondary school brought knowledge of Massinissa and Jugurtha, Berber-speaking leaders of rebellion against Carthage and Rome in the second century B.C., (in Sallust), as well as the story of the French Revolution. Others had been oppressed, Hadjeres found out, and had done something about it. But this awareness never interfered with a growing love of French culture. Especially impressive to him and his friends was a socialist professor who sympathized with their embryonic nationalism, yet was able to make the students love France. One of this professor's students was Ali Boumendjel, Hadjeres recalls, who was grateful to this teacher to his dying day, the day when Ali was tortured to death by French parachutists.

Before, during, and after the war, revolutionary discussion became more intense; the Manifesto of 1943 was read; cultural circles were opened; Arabic schools were encouraged; Arabic terms that had lain buried were used again; and radios were bought only after it was made sure that they carried Near Eastern stations. The eve of struggle for independence had been reached.

Hadjeres then describes the state of Algerian culture in 1961 as a polylinguistic mosaic. He tells of Algerian youths who spoke Berber in the bosom of their families, Arabic on the road, and French in primary school. The ALN meetings, especially on the commander level, were held in French while talks on the base level were in Arabic or Berber, and sometimes in French. The future, Hadjeres writes, demands an education of an Arab-Islamic sort with French culture and language restricted to a subordinate position, although one relatively more important than those of other foreign cultures. The cultivated man, Hadjeres writes, will be one who "is instructed in both Arabic and French," and French, as a second language, "will play, with the culture it is a medium for, a far more brilliant role than during the somber period when French was an official and imposed language." From Hadjeres' view of the future, there appears to be substantial truth in the remark sometimes made that the French are among the most ineffective colonial powers from a political point of view, but unrivalled from the cultural point of view.

Among outstanding Algerian leaders, the *évolué* last to repudiate the ideal of assimilation was Ferhat Abbas, the president of the Provisional Government of the Algerian Republic until the summer of 1961. His final repudiation of assimilation, as late as the Second World War, was a testimony to the success of this policy but a sign that this ideal of assimilation had lost appeal in its last stronghold among the North African Moslems.

In the pre-World War II period a characteristic debate among educated Moslems was that of Islamization versus modernization and frenchification, that is, whether Moslems should work toward an independent Algeria reconstructed according to the precepts of the Koran or whether they should opt for the complete political and cultural assimilation of Algeria to the French Republic. Ferhat Abbas before the Second World War was a proponent of the second point of view, and significantly his colleagues (at least in the summer of 1960) in the FLN instead of trying to deny what might seem to be this embarrassing past allegiance, used it to justify their choice for revolution. France, they maintained, once had the chance of winning the loyalty of men like Abbas. It failed to do so, and therefore an Abbas had no alternative but to choose the way of revolution to win dignity and equality for himself and for his compatriots.

Abbas, while a young man studying at the University of Algiers, gave expression to his thoughts and sentiments in a number of newspaper articles which he later gathered together and published under the title *Le jeune algérien*. The work abounds in references to French literature — the opening quotation is from Pascal — and some of the articles included were originally published under the pen name Kemal Abencerages, indicating his identification with a Chateaubriand hero as well as with the modernizer of modern Turkey. The theme that runs through the articles is one of love for France and for French culture but of bitterness at the failure of France, and especially of the *colons*, to allow the Algerians equality and dignity as full-fledged Frenchmen. Although his conception of Islam is a broad and liberal one, yet he insisted that the Moslems should be allowed to retain their status as Moslems because this was a part of their identity. He denied that there was anything incompatible between an allegiance to the religion of Islam and an allegiance to the French nation. His great disappointment was that France had failed to implement a policy that would result in ". . . the marriage of the Occident and the Orient . . . the reconciliation of France and Islam . . . the formation through French-Moslem culture of an oriental France that would have been the most beautiful creation of modern times." This ideal creation would represent "a loyal entente between Islam and France, between our spiritual father-land and of our intellectual fatherland." Arabic, the language of the Algerian masses and of Islam should be taught, he insisted, but to modernize and frenchify, France should make use of "a powerful lever: the language of Corneille and of Racine. . . ." The Romans, he observed, had come as conquerors to North Africa and nothing remained of their work but ruins. The Arabs, on the other hand, had come as religious crusaders and they had conquered the hearts of the people. France, he stated, should behave in North Africa as the Arabs had, and not in the spirit of the Romans. And appealing to France, Abbas declared: "Help us to reconquer our dignity or else take back your schools." [23]

The final political status of Algeria which Abbas envisioned would be that of a French province — the title for his completed collection of articles was "De la colonie vers la province." While this province of Algeria would be principally Moslem in religion, it would be politically and academically a part of metropolitan France. Abbas, as late as 1936, rejected the idea of an Algerian nation as a myth and a delusion. In that year he published an article entitled "France — That's Myself" in which he made his frequently quoted statement: "There is no such thing as an Algerian Fatherland. I have not been able to discover it. I have examined its history; I have questioned the living and the dead; I have walked through cemeteries; nobody talked to me about it. . . . We are the children of a new world, a creation of the French mind and of French energy." [24] Abbas was answered most forcibly not by other évolués, but in Esh-Shihab (The Meteor), a journal of the reformist Ulema of Algeria, a group opposed to French education, to the idea of assimilation, and to Western rationalism, all in the name of Pan-Arabism and Islam. "We also," the Ulema leader Sheikh Ben Bades stated, "have searched in history and in the present, and we have ascertained that an Algerian Moslem nation existed and still exists . . . and it is not France, cannot be France, and no longer wishes to be France." [25]

The most hopeful sign that France might accede to the hopes and demands of Abbas and other assimilationists was the Popular Front's project of 1936–37, known as the Blum-Viollette Bill. This bill would have extended full French citizenship to certain categories of Algerian Moslems who because of their standard of education, their contributions to civil administration, or their military service, had proven themselves deserving. At the same time this bill provided that these Moslems could retain their Moslem civil status, and so remain members of the Moslem religious community. The assimilationists supported this bill as the first step towards the eventual assimilation of all Algerian Moslems to the French city. Their support for the bill was as ardent as their disillusionment was great when the *colons* prevented the bill from even reaching the stage of parliamentary debate. The fiasco of the Blum-Viollette Bill caused men like Abbas to question seriously for the first time the possibility of assimilation. But they continued to have faith that ultimately France would realize the wisdom and generosity of the socialist policy of Léon Blum and Maurice Viollette, and overcome the opposition of the *colons* and of the French Right. As late as 1940, the sensitive observer Charles-André Julien observed that many Algerian intellectuals, in contrast to their Moroccan and Tunisian counterparts, still favored and demanded political assimilation. Julien, however, warned that France must respond positively and rapidly to the demands of these educated Moslems, or forfeit her only hope of retaining their loyalty.[26] France failed to make this response and by the end of the Second World War, Abbas, having lost his faith that assimilation was either possible or desirable, advocated Algerian political autonomy. But even then, as disillusioned as he had become in France, he did not support full independence. The motto of his party was: "Neither assimilation, nor new masters, nor separation." [27]

At this time the radical movement was directed by Messali Hadj, who had cut the silver cord completely and was advocating: "National Union and a free Algeria, sovereign and independent." [28] But although Abbas still hoped for close ties with France in 1946 he had come to agree with both the extremist Messali Hadj and the reformist Ulema that there now existed an Algerian nation that could no longer constitute a part of France. On August 23, 1946, he declared in the French National Assembly: "The Algerian personality, the Algerian fatherland, which I was unable to discover among the Moslem masses in 1936, I have discovered today. . . ." [29] This statement rang the death knell to the one-time possibility that at least a part of the Moslem elite

of Algeria could have been assimilated to France. By 1960 Abbas
was using the characteristic language of the Algerian nationalists.
At the Fourth Congress of the Moslem Algerian Students' Union,
for example, he denounced colonialism for "preventing us from
learning our own language," and for having destroyed "our national culture."

VI

ANTI-FRENCH LITERATURE IN FRENCH

The most remarkable expression of French culture in North Africa is probably the school of Jewish and Moslem writers that appeared after the Second World War. This literary movement is remarkable, however, not only as a tribute to the French policy of assimilation. It also constitutes ironically, in its themes and in its subject matter, a repudiation of France and of the ideal of assimilation. This North African literature of protest and revolt, though inspired with the spirit of the French literary tradition and although written in French, is deeply opposed to French political and cultural colonialism.[1]

The North African writers have produced poetry and drama of excellence, but their major medium of expression has been the novel. The most productive center has been Algeria where, encouraged by *colon* writers originally (Emmanuel Roblès, Albert Camus and others), Mohammed Dib, Mouloud Feraoun, and Mouloud Mammeri published their first novels in the years 1952–53. Since then a large number of other writers have appeared. Among them is Assia Djebar, the first Algerian Moslem woman to write novels, and Albert Memmi, a Tunisian Jew, who identified himself, or at least tried to, with the Arab Moslem intelligentsia. The main literary modes that have appeared so far are those of the older descriptive novelists whose works have a revolutionary content (Mammeri, Dib), and those of the younger school of writers like Kateb Yacine who are more explorative, more original, and who tend to express themselves symbolistically.[2] The latter group, Yacine in particular, are sometimes too advanced in their technique to reach more than a small part of the audience to which they address themselves.

The setting of most of their works is the city or village life, Arab or Berber, of North Africa. The themes are mostly pessimistic and reflect the tensions and violence of contemporary Algerian life. In Dib's *La grande maison*, Omar, the hero as a child, lives with constant hunger in Tlemcen. In *L'incendie*, the second of the three-volume cycle, Omar is pictured growing up in a village in which the peasantry is on the verge of revolution against the *colons* who have taken their best lands.[3] Feraoun, in his *La terre et le sang* deals with the bitter and vengeful legacy of the past as it works in a Berber village. The hero, who once in France accidentally killed a member of another clan, is brutally murdered when he returns to his village. In the poetic drama *Le cercle de représailles*, Yacine tells of the torture by the French and then the murder by a conservative relative (a symbol of collaboration and resignation) of a revolutionary hero. The assassin, in this symbolic poetic drama, is finally slain by the spirit of the ancestors symbolized by a vulture. Assia Djebar in *Les impatients* treats of a young Moslem woman who rebels ineffectively against the conservative spirit of both her family and of herself. Malek Haddad and Henri Kréa as well as Yacine write about the Algerian revolution. And one other theme that appears in the works of these writers is that of the plight of the sensitive *évolué* in this world of rapid change, turmoil, and quest for identity. It is of this last theme that some elaboration will be made.

Malek Haddad, in his *L'élève et la leçon*, touches upon the dilemmas of several Algerian *évolués* during the period of the present Algerian revolution. The book reports the reveries and reminiscences of an elderly Algerian doctor in France. The occasion is a conversation between him and his daughter. He is pained to find that after years of separation she only wants from him an abortion and a haven for her boy friend, who is an Algerian rebel. The doctor finds it ironical that this girl, smoking a Gauloise, speaking perfect French, better-read in Martin du Gard than in Dib or Yacine, should sacrifice her child on behalf of this revolution. The excursion into the past, which his daughter's presence has inspired, takes him back to his life as a young doctor in an Algerian town. He recalls having been shunned by the *colons* in Algeria even when the European doctor was out of town. Glancing at his daughter's school notebook, in which she as a child copied out her lessons, he is both amused and moved to read: "Les Sarrasins étaient des guerriers courageux et cruels. . . . Mais Roland sonna si fort du cor. . . ." He is reminded of a teacher he once had, an Algerian who loved France and obtained French citizenship. The teacher had been condemned by his friends as a "m'tourni," a person who has renounced his own people. In fact, however, this teacher had been sincerely convinced of both the greatness of Islam's past and of the necessity of making Algeria wholly French. Later in life, the doctor learned that his teacher's ideal had been the "projet Blum-Viollette." [4]

Dib's three-volume cycle has as its protagonist a young boy of sensitivity and insight who grows up in the slums of Tlemcen. Through the boy's eyes one sees Algeria, both country and city, on the eve of revolt against France and against terrible conditions of social and economic injustice (Dib, like many of his colleagues is a leftist as well as a nationalist). One of Omar's earliest experiences occurs at his school in Tlemcen, when M. Hassan, the instructor, announces "the Motherland" as the topic for the day. "Who of you can tell me what the word Motherland means?" asks the teacher. Embarrassed silence follows until one student says: "France is our Motherland." This breaks the silence and all the students begin to chatter except for Omar who broods: "France, capital Paris. He knew that. The French one saw in the roads came from there. To go there and back one took a boat . . . one crossed the Mediterranean. He had never seen a boat or the sea . . . France, a pattern in many colors. How could this faraway land be his mother? His mother is at home; it is Aini; there weren't two. Aini is not France. Nothing in common. Omar had discovered a lie. Motherland or not motherland it was not his mother. He was learning ideas to escape the famous olive-wood switch. . . ." The teacher goes on to explain what a patriot is. Omar wonders whether M. Hassan or the revolutionary, Hamid Saraj, whom the police are looking for, is the patriot. Suddenly he is awakened from his revery to hear the teacher speaking in Arabic. Although he knows M. Hassan is a Moslem he had no idea that he could speak Arabic. Hassan in a low voice marked with intensity tells the students: "It isn't true when they tell you France is your Motherland." The teacher sits down, is agitated, thinks of saying something else but restrains himself. So, writes Dib, "he failed to teach his students what their Motherland was."

In Dib's *L'incendie* Omar lives with a relative in the countryside, in a poor village. Here he learns more about the conditions of his life, becomes sensitive to his difference from the French *colons*. He refuses, for example, to join in stealing from them: "He didn't steal; he didn't want to steal, especially from the Europeans: he wished, he said, to be able to look them in the eyes. The Europeans naturally preferred to deal with Arabs who stole.

Omar wished to behave and to talk like a man. . . ." Later he has an experience which makes him even more aware of the gulf that separates him from the French ruling class. He is whistled at by a Frenchman who asks him to carry some things to the house. Omar, although he speaks some French, is tongue-tied, too embarrassed to inform the Frenchman that he is not a porter. Omar does as he is asked. He follows the man and his son, with the heavy load on his arm. He is afraid to be seen by his friends who would laugh at him. They finally arrive at the villa and the man gives Omar a franc and then asks him a few questions about his name and age. "You see, Jean-Pierre," the man tells his son, "this boy is almost the same age as you." Then the man asks where Omar has learned French and Omar tells him at a school which he has had to leave. Making an example of this, the father informs his son of the fact that Omar has had to leave school in order to work. Other questions follow until the man becomes embarrassed as to what to say next. He offers Omar his son's picture book as a present, but Jean-Pierre begins to scream that the book is his. The father scolds his son, tells him to remember that many children have no books at all, that they have to work. Little Jean-Pierre again cries out that the book is his. "Yes it's yours," the father sighs. He looks at his watch. "Be on your way, little one," he says to Omar. He opens the door and Omar crosses the threshold and departs.

Concerned with the dilemma of the French-educated intellectual who finds that he belongs neither to the French world nor to his native world are the two novels of the Tunisian Jew, Albert Memmi, and the Algerian Moslem, Mouloud Mammeri. Albert Memmi's *La statue de sel* is largely autobiographical. It tells the story of a boy from a poor Jewish community in Tunis who has the good fortune to receive an education in French schools but only to find, upon maturing, that he has lost his roots in his own traditionalist community, is denied entrance to the French world, and is unable to identify himself with the revolutionary Moslems fighting for their independence.[5] After a period of rootlessness and solitude, he finally is able to see himself objectively and to accept his lot with understanding and dignity. The bulk of the book is concerned with the hero's youthful experiences in self-discovery.[6]

At his French *lycée*, the protagonist is impressed by the principal "because of his perfect diction and polished manners that represented, for us, the real Frenchman from metropolitan France whose prestige remains undiminished." He is especially proud, once in class, when he is the only one to answer a question posed about a passage from Racine: "I, son of an Italian-Jewish father and a Berber mother, had discovered in Racine's work the line that is most typical of Racine." Rousseau in particular means something to him: "I felt that I could recognize in his passion and his humble background, in his rejection of his own surroundings, my own future." He deeply resents certain teachers who are nationalistic, anti-Semitic, and anti-Arab. A mathematics teacher humiliates Jews and Moslems in class when they make mistakes by crying out to the amusement of the European students: "This is the voice of Africa calling!" During the days of Pétain he is shocked to experience anti-Semitic laws imposed by the government of the country he has been taught to identify himself with and when he finds himself in trouble with the police, he receives no real help from his French friends. He is rejected when he tries to volunteer, later, to fight in the liberation of France. He returns to school after the war but cannot take his studies seriously any more; he departs with a friend to Argentina to begin a new life.

Mouloud Mammeri's *Le sommeil du juste* has as its protagonist a sensitive, poetic young man named Arezki who grows up in a Berber village. His background is a miserable one of family vendettas and of primitive prejudices. Much of the book consists of a long letter from Arezki, in prison for a crime he did not commit, to his old French tutor. He tells the tutor that it was at his hands that he, the student, first became conscious of himself as a person and learned the humanistic values that he had when he entered the war as a soldier to fight for France. In the army, however, he found that French soldiers were favored over Arabs, and he began to feel, after a series of unhappy experiences, that he would never be able to enter the French city freely. He would always be regarded as an outsider. He describes a drunken scene, a symbolic orgy, when he sets fire to a batch of books including some by Molière and Montesquieu; his disillusionment will prevent him from becoming a teacher and teaching what he no longer believes. The book ends when he returns to his village to hear his brother tell him resignedly: "You must know that it's all over with, that everything's over, finished, since you won the war. The old order has come into its own again. . . ." As if to confirm this, Arezki is unjustly sentenced to twenty years in prison by a French provincial judge who has slept through most of the trial.

By 1954 many Algerians had concluded that the old had indeed come into its own again, but that this time they would reject it. Helped by these artists who were French educated and who wrote in French, they had discovered their "otherness," they were in search now of their own proper identity.

Would the rejection of cultural assimilation to France by these writers mean the demise of this extraordinary school of French literature? Many of these writers appeared to believe so. Thus Albert Memmi has written: "The literature of the colonized in a European language seems condemned to die young." [7] Malek Haddad once wrote: "I who sing in French, my friend, if my accent should shock you, remember that colonialism has inflicted this defect upon me." [8] Jean Senac considers that his literary work is only a transcription or, at best, a translation of North African life, and he has referred to himself and his colleagues as "writers of transition." [9] And most sweeping in his prediction is Jean Amrouche who has written: "I am a cultural hybrid. Cultural hybrids are very interesting monsters, but monsters with no future. I consider myself, therefore, condemned by history." [10] There are trained Orientalists who share this pessimism. They argue that in the relatively near future Islamic-Arab culture will submerge the French element and that the school of North African writers of French expression will some day appear like a "hothouse flower" as one of them put it. Another expressed the same sentiment with the remark: "Poor Bourguiba, he thinks he can persuade the Tunisians that they are French."

But there are educators and intellectuals whose attitudes might lead one to suspect that the pessimism of the authors quoted above is premature. In Tunisia, educators often emphasize their deep attachment to French culture and their conviction that Tunisian culture must not fold in upon itself and lose contact with a mainspring of modern culture.[11] André Demeerseman, a life-long student of Tunisian culture, considers the following remark by a young Tunisian to be representative: "You Europeans only enjoy European music and writers. The Egyptians only enjoy music and writers of Arabic expression. We Tunisians love Mozart and Arabic melodies, Pascal and Taha Hossein, equally." [12] The leader of the progressive *Union Nationale des Forces Populaires*, El Mehdi Ben Barka, once told an interviewer: "It is certain that, for us, French culture constitutes a bridge between our national culture and modern technology to which the French language gives us access at present. . . . [The] place that French culture can continue to occupy will always be a place of choice." [13] Hadjeres, as indicated in a previous chapter, appears to believe that French will play as important a role in an independent Algeria as Ben Barka believes it will play in Morocco, and even Malek Haddad, the most violent critic of assimilation, has said: "When peace and liberty are given to my fatherland, I will be able to say that my love for the Arabs is not incompatible with the emotion that Vercors arouses in me." [14]

The question of the future of French culture in North Africa is not closed, then. It may be that North African writers will only write in Arabic in the future, but the cultural and spiritual values that Albert Camus and his Moslem friends have had in common may survive in North Africa. Were this not to happen, both Arabs and French would lose, and the fault would lie in part in the sad errors and belated decisions made in the devolution of an empire, yesterday and today.

VII

AMBIVALENT ATTITUDES OF *ÉVOLUÉS* AND THE PROBLEM OF IDENTITY

In rebelling against colonial domination, the colonized seek to repudiate the inferior social and psychological status once imposed upon them. They wish to assert their own identity and to prove to themselves and to others that they are capable of self-government and of progress without the paternalistic guidance of the colonial power. Once independent they will tend naturally to erase the symbols of colonial supremacy, and also the symbols of the "backwardness" which made it possible for a foreign power to conquer and to dominate them. Their policy, after independence is won, will therefore be two-fold, and in a sense contradictory.

This dual policy has been followed in Tunisia and Morocco since their attainment of independence in 1956. On the one hand overt and dramatic symbols of the French domination have been eliminated.[1] The giant statue of General Lyautey on horseback in Casablanca has been removed to the garden of the French consulate and his remains which once rested in a beautiful native-type tomb in Rabat now lie in the Invalides. In Tunis the monumental statues of Cardinal Lavigerie and Jules Ferry no longer stand at either end of the central avenue which was once called Jules Ferry and now is Habib Bourguiba Avenue. On the other hand, in Tunisia the government has not hesitated to demolish old Turkish walls or to consider clearing out the charming *suqs* of Tunis and of other cities in order to build large avenues and improve hygiene. As a French resident of Tunis said: "What we consider to be quaint and charming, a beautiful legacy from the past, they consider to be symbols of backwardness. What we preserved for them out of respect for their traditions, they see as symbols of the backwardness in which we tried to keep them." [2]

The ambivalence that one finds among so many *évolués* in

North Africa today, toward the culture of their former colonizer and toward their own proper past, is an understandable product of the colonial period. The colonized were made to feel that there must be something wrong with their traditional culture, and so with themselves, or else they would not have been dominated for so long.[3] This complex was reinforced in a variety of ways. The French tended to disparage and to suppress that part of traditional culture which they considered dangerous, and they tended to encourage that part of this culture which they could make use of or which they considered attractive but harmless.[4] They also tended to belittle the administrative ability of the "native" and to deny him positions of responsibility that might have inspired self-confidence and offered the native administrative experience.[5] The *colons*, as suggested above, added to the complex of the Moslem Arab by their racial intolerance. And, positively, many *évolués* were seduced by their education to believe in the superiority of French culture and, as a result, in the relative inferiority of their own.

That colonialism produces a "complex of inadequacy" among colonized people is perhaps obvious. That the colonized understands this fact and can observe it objectively, however, deserves attention. Two interesting studies of what might be called "the mentality of the colonized" are the two works already cited, *Portrait du colonisé* by Albert Memmi and *Vocation de l'Islam* by Malek Bennabi. Generally, the two writers come to similar conclusions about the mentality of the colonized, though they differ as to its origin. Memmi traces the cause to imperialism which he condemns out of hand, and Bennabi, though of course attributing much to imperialism, ascribes the cause to the "colonisabilité" of the native. Both writers agree as to the image which serves to justify political domination. The native is lazy, unchangeable but amusing; he is weak and needs protection from himself and from others; his one virtue, hospitality, proves his stupidity; he is an opaque object ("they are all the same. . . ."). The colonizer persuades the native of this image of himself by segregating him from the "new city," and isolating him in a world of frozen customs and traditions. In school, if the colonized is among the minority to enter, he is taught from another's memory and so he becomes unhistorical and a stranger in his own country. Conversely, the *évolué* is never really accepted by the *colon*; his tone is never perfect, he is made to feel imitative. Memmi feels it is significant that the leaders of the revolutionary movements against France — Abbas, Bourguiba, Messali Hadj and others — lost their faith in assimilation only after having attempted to become as French as possible, and that they believed that to find themselves, their own beings as men, they must rebel and be Arabs.[6] However, even in revolt and even with independence, the *colonisé* finds himself in an ambiguous position. He has been convinced by the presence of the colonizers of the inferiority of his past and yet it is to this that he claims to be returning. To attain a genuine sense of identity, the *évolué* must struggle for a long time to turn negative revolt into a positive affirmation of the self he is still seeking to find. Bennabi observes that many *évolués* are the victims of an upbringing which makes them only superficially modern and only superficially Moslem. They have discovered only the utilitarian side of Western culture and not the spiritual and intellectual center which has made utilitarian success possible. They confuse means and ends. On the other hand, they tend to see their own Islamic culture in its uncreative, ossified, passive side — that which made it possible for the Arabs to be easily dominated in the past. And in repudiating assimilation to the West, these *évolués* defend the worst of their traditional culture instead of the principles of rationalism and humanism which once made Islam a dynamic and creative culture. They confuse the word, the symbol, with the reality that once lay behind it. Their responsibility, their "vocation," is to rediscover the reality rather than only the form of their past, and the reality and not only the surface of the modern Western world. For Bennabi then, the new identity that must be created in North Africa is to be a synthesis of what is valuable both in Islam and in the West.

To create this new identity, however, on a more than superficial and synthetic level, is, of course, a difficult and complex task. Many North African *évolués* would readily agree with Bennabi's diagnosis and prescription, but, in practice, they are unsure as to how to modernize their countries and at the same time give vitality to the values and institutions of the traditional culture of their nations, to the world of the *medina* and of orthodox and popular Islam. They are uncertain how to modernize without losing themselves,[7] and, conversely, how to revitalize the culture of the masses and of Islam without the forfeiture of, or at least the delay in, becoming as progressive as they consider a nation such as France to be. This uncertainty, this ambivalence, can be seen in the policies they prescribe for their nations, and it can be seen on a personal, "existential," level, in the mind and soul of the individual *évolué*. His is often the problem of the "marginal man," the person who belongs to two cultures but cannot completely identify with either.[8] He may see himself as a victim of history, as a person who has become too French in his habits and in his psychological make-up ever to be able, or even willing, to identify himself with the masses of his people. And with independence, he may do what he can to assure that his children will never suffer the embarrassment of administrators of his generation who are unable to communicate in Arabic, or artists like Haddad, who feel themselves to be in the "exile" of the French language. But at the same time, and even though he may know that France is no longer "la grande nation," he often tends to believe that a knowledge of French will be needed as a bridge to the world of the twentieth century, and he is still attached to French cultural values. It is not untypical that Bourguiba, for example, should have difficulty in believing that a man who does not speak fluent French can be really cultivated.[9] And it is not strange that today's governing nationalists of Tunisia and Morocco, though dedicated to arabization, should give to the French language an important and perhaps even a preponderant role in the upbringing of the young, and that the new system of education of these nations should continue to reflect the spirit and the organization of the French system of education.

This allegiance to French education, however, this reluctance to transform the education system radically, and the present compromise that is bilingual and bicultural leave the education reformers of Morocco and Tunisia with a host of perplexing questions. How much French should be taught, for example? To what extent should the French system of education which aims, at the higher levels, at producing quality rather than quantity, be revised to meet the needs of under-developed countries? Can children who are educated bilingually become anything more than "marginal" men? And, conversely, will children who are educated bilingually lose the advantages of their parents who have a familiar and easy access to a rich, sophisticated foreign culture?

In addition to the question of integrating Moslem and French culture, the North African leaders have other problems affecting the quest for individual and national identity. One such challenge is that of cultural disunity and diversity which is the source of many divisive political tendencies and which will continue to render many purely political solutions to current North African problems vain. In Morocco, and to a lesser degree in Algeria, an obstacle to unity will continue to be the Berber heritage of a great proportion of the people. In parts of the Atlas Mountains there are Berbers who speak no Arabic and who in their customs continue to resist the Arabic culture of the cities. Berberism has survived many conquerors and some students of the subject believe that its stubborn individuality, though misjudged by the French as an ally, is likely to offer a profound resistance to any effort to completely arabize the area.[10] Another question is the depth of the unconscious allegiance of the mass of the peoples of North Africa to an often superstitious and uninformed Islam; it will not be easy for the orthodox religious reformers to erase Maraboutism or for the Kemalists to modernize their countries rapidly.[11] And a problem, relevant to Morocco only, is presented by the loyalty of the masses to the person of the monarch who claims descent from the Prophet's family and is the possessor of *baraka* (the power to grant grace). Monarchy may be the only significant factor for national unity, but it happens that an influential part of the elite is republican in sympathy if not in principle, and may strive for unity, one day, with the republican states of Algeria and Tunisia.[12]

Although compared to Morocco, Tunisia impresses the observer as a homogeneous and united nation, it also is not free from the difficulties of what the progressives might consider to be "culture lag." For example, in 1960 Bourguiba asked his people to abandon the custom of fasting during the month of Ramadan in order to be able to work more effectively for their country. He argued that this was fully compatible with Islam in its deepest meaning and that the struggle against under-development was a form of jihad (holy war).[13] There was resistance and opposition to this thesis and many Moslems fasted in spite of the universal popularity of the President. Bourguiba, however, showed his sense of moderation and flexibility by avoiding the use of force and limiting himself to the tactic of persuasion. He was aware that his people would not follow him blindly when they were asked to deny one of their deepest traditions.

The two cases, of monarchy in Morocco and Ramadan in Tunisia, illustrate some of the tensions in contemporary North Africa; they point to the problem of effecting genuine progress while at the same time retaining national unity and cohesion. They also illustrate the general fact confronting North African leaders, that unity and progress depend ultimately upon the slowly changing and stubborn forces of culture rather than on the easier and more rapid changes that political action can effect. It is for this reason that the victories of the *évolués* must be won in the classrooms of North Africa as well as in the political arena.[14]

Related to the problem of national and cultural unity is the problem of individual identity, of resolving the contradictory impulses of the individual *évolué* in whose bosom some of the tensions which beset his nation find an internal psychological and spiritual expression. The purely French-educated *évolué* in North Africa tends to feel uncomfortable in traditional Islam.[15] He finds it as difficult to accept the orthodox fundamentalism of the reformists as to respect the Maraboutism of the masses. At the same time he wishes to identify with his people culturally and religiously. But the progressive view of Islam that he will often advocate, the notion that "real" Islam and modernism are fully compatible, is unacceptable or strange to the masses of his compatriots and to their traditional religious mentors.[16]

As well as feeling ill at ease in the religious traditions of his society, the *évolué* can also feel a sense of guilt at being culturally too French in his habits and tastes.[17] This concern appears, for example, in a letter written to *Afrique-Action* (February 13, 1961) by a Tunisian student. "My feeling when I read *Afrique-Action*," he stated, "is that of a young Tunisian who is reading a foreign periodical that treats of African problems and particularly of Tunisian problems." He went on to say that he did not consider the periodical "foreign" because it was published in the French language, but because of the patronizing tone of its writers (most of whom were Tunisians). These writers, he said, "deal with the different problems of this young country with a certain air of more or less disguised paternalism," and he accused them of tending to "depersonalize" their readers and of discouraging these readers from drawing upon sources that were "authentically Tunisian." The editor answered that while it was worthy to wish to be "oneself," one should draw upon all sources, foreign or native, which enrich one's personality. He might have observed also that it was not very easy to know what is "authentically Tunisian." Contemplating his native culture, the hero of Memmi's novel, *La statue de sel*, declared: "When I learned some history I suffered from vertigo; Phoenicians, Romans, Vandals, Byzantines, Berbers, Arabs, Spanish, Turks, Italians, French, I forget them all and get them confused. Five hundred steps (in Tunis) and one changes civilization." Perhaps the editor could then have suggested to the student that he should be proud that a part of what is authentically Tunisian is its rich and variegated heritage, but the student, like Memmi's hero, would probably have found this unhelpful as well as paternalistic. Yet a sympathetic outside observer, at least a Westerner, would like to think that Tunisia, and North Africa, will be able to preserve as much of this pre-Western heritage as is consonant with social progress and national unity. The Maghreb, lying between the Middle East, Africa, and the Latin West, may have a creative and individual role to play in the years ahead, a role which will be "authentic" and with which the educated elite can identify with pride. This, in any case, is the challenge. The elimination of "cultural oppression" is only a beginning; the problem now is to give political freedom a positive spiritual content, to free both the citizen and the person.

In the summer of 1960 the author had the opportunity of discussing the various aspects of the cultural problem of identity and unity with a number of intellectuals in Morocco and Tunisia. Their answers to the problems that remain to be solved after independence were different, but they all illustrated with what ambivalence *évolués* face the French cultural presence and how real is the problem of identity.

A prominent young journalist observed that it was not strange that Tunisians did most of their newspaper reading in French rather than in Arabic. The explanation lay in the character of education under the French. "Our generation," he said, "thinks in French and it is very difficult for me, for example, even though I am a graduate of Sadiqi, to adjust myself to thinking in Arabic. As editor of an Arabic newspaper and as a party militant of the Neo-Destour, this is frustrating." In Sadiqi, he stated, Arabic was used for language and civilization studies, while all the modern subjects were taught in French. Very few of his generation have been able, like Messadi, to attain to a complete and spontaneous mastery of Arabic.[18] The greatest intellectual and literary influences in the country, he said, were Western through the French medium. "We know Hemingway and Faulkner as well as Camus this way, we are not restricted simply to the French world. Egyptian writers of purely Arabic formation we find too simple in content. It is to the Lebanese that we feel closest," he added, "mainly because, like us, they are the product of two cultures; they are open to the Western world as are we."

The director of a Tunisian primary school of two hundred students, who had received his elementary education in a small traditional koranic school and so had once known Arabic well, said that when he had gone to Sadiqi he had learned weak French and lost the firm grasp of Arabic he once had had. He also objected to the bilingual system in which he was obliged to teach, for it did not provide a strong grounding in either language (he preferred a completely Arabic system with French as an accessory language). He deplored the fact that his students regularly violated the regulation which limited either French or Arabic conversation to certain specified times of the school day. Although he was the director of the school, he could do little to enforce the regulation because he, himself, violated it regularly. And a thirty-year-old Tunisian in private business, trained in banking methods in both France and the United States, said that he felt at a disadvantage in independent Tunisia because his Arabic was so weak. He would not consider, for example, entering into politics.

An important French cultural officer attached to the French Embassy in Tunis expressed a French point of view of the problems of Tunisian culture. He maintained that the problem of bilingualism is nothing new, nor is the problem of having creative artists express themselves in languages other than their native tongues. He cited as examples Belgium and Switzerland, the works of Conrad and Koestler, and the fact that in Central Africa French is the common educated language as Spanish is in Mexico; he pointed to the rich literary production of the new school of Algerian writers discussed above. Where there is talent and material, he suggested, the medium can be, and is, found. Slapping a pile of that morning's newspapers lying in front of him on the desk, he said: "The problem is here, this self-conscious absorption in economic development and political organization, congresses and the rest of it, to the point of boredom. How dull it all can be! Their utilitarianism is the problem, their lack of a sense of humor, of irony, without which one suffocates. There is no concern with the important things, love, happiness. . . . How different they are from an elderly Moslem friend of mine, of the old tradition, who lives deep in the *medina* with his books and his thoughts.

He has wit and a sense of proportion. Typical of the present young elite is the wife of the Minister of Education, herself a director of a school, who visited France a short time ago. A journalist asked her to comment on problems of women in Tunisia, and even in the best of worlds women have problems! Cold and impenetrable, the minister's wife said: 'The women of Tunisia have no problems, they all support Bourguiba.' And that was That."

France of course has a vested interest in maintaining bilingualism in North Africa for as long as this is possible. An advisor to the President told the author with a twinkle in his eye that Bourguiba once in difficult negotiations had alarmed the French by a mock threat to import hundreds of English and American teachers and change the second language to English. The United States Mission, which supplied more funds to Tunisia in 1960 than did the French, was very careful not to intrude on the cultural domain of education over which they knew their ally to be so sensitive. A political officer in the United States Embassy declared that American policy was to let the French do the teaching because it would be absurd for two Western powers, with a common enemy, to engage in internecine squabbles over ways of serving a common cause. A Tunisian secondary school teacher indicated that he did not think an American type of education should replace the French system because it would produce students of lower academic and cultural quality. His objection to the Minister of Education, Messadi, was not that Messadi was completely devoted to the French system of education, but that the Minister was loyal to the French system of a quarter of a century ago. Bilingualism should remain the rule in Tunisia, this teacher maintained, because Arabic was not an adequate medium of expression in the twentieth century. On the other hand, he agreed that this dependence on France helped to explain why Tunisian culture remained a provincial reflection of French culture and had produced very little that was fresh or original.[19] It might be necessary, he said, for Tunisia to become monolingual eventually and for artists to express themselves in Arabic, as they appeared to be doing effectively in Egypt. But, he sighed, in such an arabized Tunisia there would be no place for people like himself.

As one might expect, the same ambivalence that exists toward French culture among the Tunisians is found in Morocco. Morocco, however, is less French and more Moslem and traditionalist than is Tunisia, and therefore more dependent upon French aid in "modernizing." Tunisia, for example, had only a few French doctors in 1960 and their contracts were soon to expire, while Morocco still depended on 467 French doctors; Tunisia graduated 1,000 *bacheliers* in 1960, and Morocco only 200; and historically Tunisia has always been more open to the West and more cosmopolitan than Morocco.[20]

An opportunity to sense some of the problems and prospects of young Moroccan *évolués* was given the author in 1960 by contact with two young Moroccans, one a student of agriculture in France on his way to Rabat for his holidays, and the other a thirty-two-year-old expert in communications from Oujda on his way to work in Marrakesh. These two young men will be referred to as Shawki and Ahmed.

On the aeroplane from Paris to Rabat, Shawki pointed to the sunlit brown coast line of Gibraltar and then Morocco, and the small expanse of sparkling sea that separated them. "What a small distance separates East and West," he remarked, "yet how profoundly it has done so." At the airport, Shawki was met by his brother, a Rabat lawyer. The two embraced in fluent French. Next day the author was invited to Shawki's home, a white French-built and French-furnished villa in a quiet residential area of Rabat. Shawki talked with pride about his French education but with regret about the virtual non-existence of his Arabic. He was a nationalist and deplored the fact that he could not communicate with the common man of his own nation. He hoped some day to spend a year in Egypt in order to "arabize" himself as he put it. He spoke with love of France where he had never experienced any racial discrimination. He felt irritation, however, when his French classmates disparaged the Moroccans for studying humanities in preference to the more rigorous sciences. Young Moroccans today, Shawki insisted, were entering technical fields and they would prove to the French that they had the capacity for serious work in complex modern fields.

In contrast to Shawki who spoke poor Arabic and who called himself a Kemalist religiously, Ahmed knew Arabic very well and described himself as a convinced Moslem. His father had persuaded him to learn Arabic at the same time that he was pursuing his studies in French. When Ahmed met an old schoolmate, the two conversed in Arabic and French interchangeably, although Arabic predominated. His favorite author was André Gide, he said, and his favorite newspapers *Le Monde* and *L'Express*. He expressed a great fondness for Arabic music but felt that its orchestration should be enriched with more instruments and that it should seek to combine Western with Eastern musical styles. In this regard, he expressed a great admiration for the musical contribution of the Egyptian Abdul-Wahhab. He spoke with no bitterness about the colonial past, but he felt that General Lyautey, estimable as he was, had done harm by creating a sharp division in Moroccan cities between the traditional *medina* and the "new city." A blending of the two worlds, Ahmed argued, would have helped the Moroccan people to enter the twentieth century more easily and rapidly. For Ahmed, and for so many other North African *évolués*, the problem of identity was the problem of integrating the *medina* with the *nouvelle ville*.

VIII

THE SEARCH FOR IDENTITY: ARABIZATION AND MODERNIZATION IN NORTH AFRICA

Moroccans and Tunisians, since 1956, have had the opportunity of fashioning the institutions which will mold the future identity of their children and of their nation. Decisions concerning the education of the leaders of tomorrow have already been made, and even though these decisions might be tentative compromises their effect will bear heavily upon the future. In Algeria, the war for self-determination continued until July 1962, and until then formal education was still in the hands of the French. However, the process of war itself also served indirectly to educate the Algerians to a new identity as well as to an allegiance to the new Algerian nation.

———

The Moroccan nationalists, upon the attainment of independence, sought to correct what they considered to be the faults of the system of education under the protectorate. The two major faults, they believed, had been the degree to which Moroccan culture and language had been ignored, and the extent to which young Moroccans had been denied educational opportunity. Their effort through 1961 has had four main features: it has been gradualist (in government primary schools after the first class year, 15 hours of 30 were still taught in French, and in secondary schools only 13 out of 33 hours were taught in Arabic); it has sought to increase the use of Arabic and the teaching of Moroccan and Islamic culture; it has aimed at providing universal schooling; and it has been in the process of forcing the traditional universities to modernize.

The Ministry of Education consists of a number of branches under the general direction of the Minister himself. There are, apart from the administrative branch, a branch for primary education, one for secondary, and one for traditional and higher education. One had the impression in 1960 of great concern and energetic dedication to reform and an absence of any xenophobia or fanaticism. In contrast to Tunisia, however, where the counterparts of the Moroccan educators seemed surer of themselves and better organized, one had a sense in Morocco of groping and of experimentation. The ultimate goal is to create a modern, Arabic system of education to replace French and traditional education, and to unify the final product and extend it in a uniform manner to all Moroccans. Because of a paucity of teachers, especially teachers who can teach in Arabic, foreign sources are tapped.[1] As one Moroccan educator said: "We modernize and we invite Egyptian and Lebanese teachers to help us arabize. In principle, French is no more important to us than any other foreign language; we do not feel in any way committed to French. . . . Practically, however, it must remain the major foreign language for the time being."

A director of Moroccan traditional and higher education had been educated both in the French system and in the traditional system. He is the author of several books dealing with Maghreb civilization; his thesis is that Islam must be revitalized, as well as modernized, to compete in the modern world. In the fourteenth century Moroccan culture had still been creative and still equal to anything in the West, the director observed in an interview in 1960, but then came centuries of relative sterility while the West was advancing with progressively greater speed. Today Morocco must catch up, and the task is formidable. This requires the modernization of Qarawiyin University and of the other fourteen institutions which taught traditional education, and the arabization of the modern system of education with the help of other parts of the Arab world, Egypt in particular. Arabization is absolutely necessary, the director maintained,[2] if Morocco is to rediscover her Arabic and Islamic personality. But this rediscovery is to take place in a modern context. "We are not fanatics," he insisted, "we want to enter the modern world." Particularly difficult is the problem of presenting science in Arabic, in view of the rapidity of Western progress and the multiplication of new terms. Important efforts, however, are being made toward standardizing Arabic in Morocco as well as throughout the Arabic world. Arabic is to be enriched with modern terms, and thought is being given to ways of popularizing science through the production of modern, attractive, and cheap works on popular science. Until enough teachers have been trained in Arabic, foreign teachers will have to be used, but the director hopes that by 1963 the new State Normal School will have produced enough trained Moroccans to dispense with foreign teachers. Another hope is that Morocco will be able to offer its own medical degrees by the same year and that soon higher degrees will be available in modern jurisprudence, political science, and Moslem law.

The director's attitude toward French educational policy under the protectorate was critical but not bitter. "The French," he admitted, "did one thing very well. Those they educated became genuinely Western in their culture and in their outlook. Unfortunately, however, they became less Arab than their fellow Moslems elsewhere and much more ignorant of our history. But as this changes, as we arabize while still keeping the most useful parts of the French system, we will produce students who will have the advantage of experience in two cultures, and the perspective of two cultures."

In a report submitted to the Twenty-third International Conference on Public Education (July 1960, in Geneva), the Moroccan Ministry of National Education outlined its five-year plan. The aim of the plan was arabization, universalization, rationalization, and the formation of technicians needed in developing the country. Up through the academic year 1959–60, schooling of various sorts had been provided to 796,801 students. Pilot-schools that were entirely arabized had been established in that part of Morocco that was Spanish. The School of Engineering was to recruit 65 students each year and by 1963 to graduate engineers entirely formed in Morocco. The process of universalizing education would be slow; in 1960 primary education served 716,394 students which was 38 per cent of the 1,900,000 children between six and fourteen. In higher education, the aim was to offer the *licence* in all branches of science at the new university in Rabat. Moroccan students numbered 200 in this faculty out of 650 students in all; 1,734 students were in the Faculty of Juridical, Economic and Social Science in 1959–60, of whom 1,367 were Moroccan (352 French and 15 other). Of these, 359 were taking their *licence* in Arabic and 560 in French. Ninety-three students were working for their *doctorats*. In the Faculty of Letters two *licences* were offered, one Moroccan and the other French. In 1960, 227 were working for the former and 720 for the latter. A degree in Classical Arabic was being worked for by 74 students.

Between 1957 and 1960 many foreign teachers had been invited to teach special courses. Among them was Taha Husayn who lectured in all the main cities of the country, Boga Istvan of the University of Budapest who lectured in Arabic on contemporary problems of Arabic literature, and Mustapha Baroudi of Damascus who discussed the renaissance of Arab administrative organization. There were 24,436 students studying at the traditional universities (in Fez and Marrakesh) and the various Islamic centers of study, and 72,457 students were in koranic schools. Modernization was to turn these schools gradually into institutions resembling the regular government schools, and emphasis would be placed on the study of science and foreign languages. The higher cycle of studies would be replaced by a faculty which would specialize in Islamic disciplines, the history of religions, and comparative law. The report concludes with the remark that 1959-60 constituted an important date in the educational policy of Morocco "whose principal objectives are the complete enrollment of children and their training as effective participants in the movement of economic and social progress in the country."

In 1961, though academic standards were not as high as under the French, the government could boast that it had placed one million children between six and fourteen in school (46 per cent of the children of this age bracket). In secondary schools there were 29,061 students; in technical schools, 17,692; in the University of Rabat, 3,218; and in the traditional Islamic schools there were 24,615.[3]

The energy of the educational reformers of Morocco was impressive, but the problems they had to face were great, as the figures cited above indicate. Other problems were suggested by a young frenchified Moroccan teacher in a *lycée* (a teacher of the French language). Though perhaps neither realistic nor fair in the excoriating criticism of the Moroccan education policy which he voiced, this young Moslem testified to the hold of the French language in Morocco. "They are confused in the Ministry," he said, "they don't know what they are doing. One day they want to arabize everything and the next day they return to French.[4] There is no adequate university in Morocco and students must learn French to be able to study in France. The upper classes send their children to French schools and if this goes on, arabization will be equivalent to lower-class status. Also, we don't have the teachers to arabize; if we rely on what Egypt has sent us we will regress rather than move forward." His solution was to establish a modern system having French as its medium of instruction, but, of course, the spirit of today's independent Morocco is against him.[5]

The contemporary Tunisian reform movement in education was inaugurated by President Bourguiba on June 25, 1958, in a speech addressed to the parents and graduating class of the Collège Sadiqi, the alma mater of the President and of many of the other leaders of modern Tunisia.[6] Founded in 1875, Sadiqi was before the French occupation the most modern educational institution in the country. It represented something of a minor cultural revival, and it now serves as the model for the new educational system proposed by the President in his speech and embodied legally in the *Journal Officiel* (dated November 4, 1958). In the opening of his speech, the President referred to Sadiqi as "the starting point of Tunisia's renaissance. . . ."[7]

The President first described the two kinds of education Tunisia had enjoyed before 1958, "Zaitouni" education (important in having preserved Tunisia's Moslem heritage) and modern French education, which provided training for the modern world but tended to denationalize its students. He then stated that Sadiqi was the synthesis of these two systems, and the model for the educational program independent Tunisia hoped to pursue. The major aims of the government, he indicated, were these: to put all children of school age into school; to unify the system of primary education under a program "able to reinforce the national character of Tunisia which is rooted in Arab culture, the Moslem religion and a past of glory"; to offer specialized training according to the aptitudes of the students and the technical needs of the country; to incorporate the traditional schools into the unified system; and to graduate state normal students able to teach in Arabic. "French," he said, "will continue to be used provisionally where Arab teachers are lacking."

The situation facing the government before its decision to inaugurate the new program was a complex one.[8] Under the protectorate, primary education had been given in several different types of schools; French, French-Arab for boys, and French-Arab for girls, modern koranic schools, and traditional koranic schools (*kuttabs*); secondary education had been given in three types of schools, *lycées* (or *collèges*) which were typical

French high schools, "Sadiqian" schools which had offered modern French education but with an important emphasis on Arabic, and a modernized Zaitouni education. In the more purely French system, the dominant one, Arabic had been treated as a foreign language, textbooks had been the same as those used in Paris, and as Tunisians observe, the study of Tunisian geography had had the same importance as the study of an area like Australia. Nationalistic pressure had persuaded the French government in 1949 to increase the teaching of Arabic in French-Arab schools to 15 hours out of 30 for the first four years of primary, and 11 to 12 out of 30 for the last three years. All the rest had been in French. The over-all purpose of the 1958 reform was to integrate and nationalize this complex galaxy of institutions and to provide, eventually, free and obligatory education to all young Tunisians on a primary level.

In 1959–60 primary education was given throughout the country according to the same unified curriculum, and by 1963 this would be true of secondary education.[9] Arabic was the only medium of instruction in the first two years of primary and in "Normal Section A" French was studied in secondary as only the most important foreign language. The principal reason for the gradualness of arabization was the lack of teachers able to teach in Arabic, as stated above. In secondary schools the previous "classical humanities" were to be replaced by a study of Arabic literature and "the inheritance of Arab-Moslem culture." In the bilingual sections of "transitory B section" the medium of instruction would remain French until adequate staff would allow this section to be transformed into "Normal Section A." The Tunisians have modified aspects of the French system of education, in particular its emphasis upon theoretical and deductive thinking, and its encyclopedic character (placing too many facts soon forgotten into the student's head). The declared aim was to effect a combination of the French system and the Anglo-Saxon system which allows earlier specialization. Partly to liberalize the French system, and partly for budgetary reasons (and to hasten the process of universalizing primary education), the Tunisian program was made shorter than that of the French. In primary school seven years of 30 hours a week, under the French system, was replaced by six years of 25 hours a week, and secondary education was limited to six years while the French system is seven. For weaker students a system of secondary education called "Terminal Intermediate Education" was created. It was a three-year program offering a technical training. For understandable reasons, the secondary curriculum included the history of North Africa, of the Berbers, of Carthage and Egypt, and in the upper secondary classes the modern Arab world was studied together with the contemporary history of the emancipation of the Asian and African peoples.[10]

The aim announced in 1958 was to make school attendance total, as indicated, within a six-year period. It was estimated that by 1969 the school-age population (between 6 and 14) would be one million and that the number of bilingual teachers, or teachers in French, would be 6,622 (in 1960 there were 2,105); the teachers in Arabic would number 8,315 (in 1960 there were 3,253). By 1968, in order to realize total enrollment, 9,579 more teachers, 12,412 new classes, and 11,769 more school structures would be needed.[11] The cost would be great but the government was committed to granting every child an education; this was declared to be the duty of the state and the right of each child. In October 1960, the government was pleased with the progress so far made: 59 per cent of the boys of school age were enrolled and 27 per cent of the girls. The number of students in secondary school was 20,323; this was 282 more than had been planned for.[12]

To the question whether Tunisia might not find itself some day with an unemployable educated class, the answer given was that the Tunisian educational policy rested on the gamble that Tunisia would be able to modernize and industrialize herself; it represented faith in the future.

The University of Tunis, founded in March 1960, is the heir to the various institutes of higher education that existed prior to 1960. Among these were the traditionalist Zaitouna University (which in 1960 had about 650 students working for the degree called *tahsil*),[13] a Center of Economic Studies, a School of Fine Arts, and the Institute of Higher Studies. The last was the largest with 1,543 students in 1960; it offered among its various degrees, *licences* in law, mathematics, physics, chemistry and Arabic. In addition there were a Teachers' Training College (established in 1956 and patterned after the French model), a National School of Administration (founded in 1949), and a Higher Agricultural College.

The university will finally consist of four faculties: letters and human sciences; mathematical, physical and natural sciences; law and political, social, and economic studies (which will include an

American-financed business school); and medicine and pharmacy (a fifth year of medicine is planned for 1968–69). In addition there will be various research institutes.

In 1960–61 the French system was still closely paralleled and in some cases French programs were maintained in place of Tunisian equivalents. Students were therefore eligible to take examinations for French degrees. Progress would be slow, largely because the number of graduates from the secondary school system was still so small (only 290 in 1958), but by 1968–70, it was estimated that the university would have 10,500 students.

Significant trends were suggested by the following figures (all refer to Moslem students): in 1952 there were 212 Moslems in the Institute of Higher Studies; in 1959 there were 1,084. In 1952, 300 university students were studying in France; in 1959, there were 1,500. In 1952 there were 600 students at Zaitouna; in 1956 this figure had risen to 884, but in 1959 the number had fallen to 650.[14] In 1956 there were 200 students in the Middle East, and by 1959 the figure had not changed (100 were in Iraq and Lebanon, and 100 in other parts of the Middle East). If these figures are an indication of trends that will continue, it might be concluded that modern education was eclipsing traditional education rapidly, and that the attraction of European universities to young Tunisians was growing, while the attraction of Arab universities in the Middle East remained constant. It might also be observed that many of the students who are sent to the Middle East to study go to Lebanon, the most Westernized and least monolingual nation of the Middle East.

The accusation has often been made that North African students avoid the more difficult fields of science (which their countries need) in favor of law and the humanities. The figures show that in 1952, in the Institute of Higher Studies, there were 47 Moslem students in science, 99 in letters, and 66 in law. But in 1959 a significant change had occurred: there were 569 in science, 252 in letters, and 263 in law.[15] Young Tunisians, it seemed, were meeting the challenge of the primacy of science in the contemporary world.

These are some of the bare facts about the new Tunisian educational program in 1960–61. Attitudes toward it by qualified observers were mixed but generally friendly. "On the whole, and in spite of various defects," the director of the competitive French Cultural Mission said, "the efforts of the Tunisians represent intelligent decolonization." But there were criticisms. The director of a primary school believed bilingualism only led to confusion; the system, he felt, should be all Arabic with French only an auxiliary tool. An economist trained in the United States felt the system was still too French, and French of a quarter of a century ago. And a highly cultivated French educational expert argued that the effort to provide mass education by lowering the number of required years and hours of instruction would lower standards dangerously and make it difficult for students trained in the new system to cross from the Tunisian to French institutions of higher learning. However, he felt the Tunisians should be praised for realizing better than the more ambitious and hasty Moroccans that their country would have to look to France to provide higher technical training for a long time.

One of the chief officials of the Ministry of Education, and one of the architects of the new educational plan, answered some of these points. He agreed that a problem would exist for students going through the Tunisian system who wished to enter French universities. "It is partly for this reason," he asserted, "that we are establishing our own university. But we don't feel that we have watered down the French system; we feel we have improved on it. Why stuff the child's head full of details such as the battles of Philip Augustus, the names of French railroad stations or, for that matter, the names of all our early rulers? The students soon forget these things." French, however, would remain of crucial importance for a long time. "In science in particular," he observed, "it is not enough to translate textbooks into a language in which modern science is not being *thought* today; it is not only a matter of translation, of inventing equivalent scientific terms in Arabic. It is a question of spirit, of attitude. Arabization will take place very slowly and only as we train people in Arabic who have also been trained bilingually and so have shared in the universal culture which is the same for all of us today. At present we couldn't arabize fully if we wanted to, since most of our teachers are French educated.[16]

This problem of language is naturally of considerable concern to Tunisians today, as it is to Moroccans. In November 1959, a University Colloquium on Modern Arabic was held at the *Maison des Associations Culturelles* in Tunis. The following were some of the views expressed: the Director of the *Ecole Normale Supérieure de Tunis*, Abdesselem, described Arabic as "a language

consisting generally of terms relative to the affective life, and of
an archaic vocabulary; . . . [a language] whose technical terms
must be created; one which hesitates to create or borrow terms
used for modern inventions and even for objects in current contemporary use; . . . [a language weakened by] an overly rigid
syntax, the absence of vowels in writing and so forth. . . ."[17]
The major problem of this language, once so creative a medium,
lay in the difference between the written and spoken language.
These were, however, he felt, slowly being brought together by
the radio and by education, and classical terms were entering into
the common stream of speech. Others at the colloquium argued
that Arabic had and could adjust to the modern world but that
much work needed to be done, and one speaker believed the
Arab Academy of Cairo to be on the verge of solving the problem of simplifying Arabic calligraphy.[18]

The problem of whether science should be taught in Arabic
or French was the subject of a special inquiry held in 1956.[19]
Professors at the modern schools warned against hasty arabization, arguing that before Arabic could be used in science, a standard terminology would have to be created and teachers capable
of teaching in Arabic be trained. Professors of the traditional
schools argued that science was already being taught in Arabic in
a few Tunisian schools, as well as in Egypt and Syria. They maintained that Arabic should be the medium of instruction in order
to give this language dignity. But those in control of educational
policy in contemporary Tunisia were from the modernist group.
Total arabization in Tunisia was unlikely to come in the near
future.[20]

Something of the spirit of the educational reformers is revealed
in an article in *Afrique-Action* concerned with the some 5,000
graduates of Zaitouna who were unemployed in 1961.[21] The author of the article, quite paternalistically, described these unemployable intellectuals as the victims of an education given to
them by parents who were conservative and anti-French. Provided only with a koranic education, these young men had neither
the knowledge of foreign languages, nor the training in modern
intellectual techniques, to be of social use. They were not even
useful as teachers of Arabic, the author stated, and although many
were being given mechanical training to render them employable,
it was difficult to teach some of them a sense of respect for punc-

tuality. So much for an institution that was one of the greatest academic centers of the world before the Renaissance.

In early October 1961, Tunisia's students returned to their schools after a dramatic and tumultuous summer vacation. Over one thousand Tunisians had been killed by French paratroopers at Bizerte, the French Cultural Mission had been withdrawn, and many of the French teachers on contract to the government had not yet returned to their posts.[22] What the future of the educational Ten-Year Plan would be, and what role French teachers and the French language would now be allowed to play in Tunisia's future, was uncertain. But one thing was sure. Many Tunisians had come to the conclusion that it was much too dangerous to place their cultural destiny in the hands of any one foreign power. Tunisian educators were now giving serious consideration to ways of breaking the virtual monopoly that the French had over their educational system. They had decided that more of their students should be sent to universities other than the French, and that aid in finances and in personnel should come from countries other than France. And many Tunisians questioned the principle of bilingualism and argued that the process of arabization should be accelerated. Bourguiba, himself, stated in a speech to the National Assembly (October 19) that the process both of decreasing the importance of French in primary schooling and of increasing the number of available Tunisian teachers, would be stepped up.[23]

The spokesman for the Tunisian *colons*, who complained bitterly that the Bizerte crisis constituted the second stage of the "défrancisation" of Tunisia, might prove to have been right.[24]

In Algeria, efforts to encourage the study of Arabic culture and language were usually frustrated by the *colon* bloc. The constitutional statute of 1947 stated, for example, that Arabic should be taught on all levels of education in Algeria. The *colons* saw to it that this adjustment to realities remained a dead letter. An official educator, speaking for the *colon* point of view, once summarized the objection to teaching Algerians in Arabic with the observation that "neither dialectical Arabic, which has only the value of a patois, nor grammatical Arabic, which is a dead language, nor modern Arabic, which is a foreign language, can constitute a compulsory subject of primary education."[25] But the wind of change, encouraged by experiments in neighboring Morocco and Tunisia, the example of Egypt with its radio broadcasts and movies, and the Algerian war itself, were having an influence in the post-war period. A process of arabization was under way.

The author discussed the question of arabization with two members of the FLN in Tunis in 1960. They spoke fluent French; they both had been educated in France, and they were both of the generation that entered the struggle for independence at the start and now occupied positions of leadership. "I belong to a French-formed generation," one of them said, "but I believe that some day leaders of my generation might have difficulty with the younger generations because of this matter of educational background. Already I notice that younger members of our organization are more Arab in their outlook than we, and though they speak French, they often do so as Swedish businessmen, say, might speak fluent English. French for them is a tool without the spiritual and psychological association it has for us, with French culture, with the French community. Men of my generation are required to use Arabic now and this causes us anxiety.[26] It requires a deliberate effort on my part to think and speak in Arabic and it is especially difficult, in public speeches, to meet the standards of our Middle Eastern counterparts. The process of arabization among the young is largely a product of the war. Originally *El-Moudjahid*[27] was printed only in French. Now it is printed in both languages and the Arabic edition outsells the French. At the beginning of the revolution we would have organized a twenty-minute broadcast with five minutes Arabic and fifteen minutes French; today it has to be the opposite."

According to the second leader, another process encouraged by the revolution was internationalization (cultural as well as political). In 1956, a strike called by Algerian Moslem university students began this second process.[28] Henceforth, progressively more Algerian students have been studying in countries other than France; ten were in the United States in 1960, some were in Iron Curtain countries,[29] and others in Cairo. Also, many students went to French-speaking countries like Switzerland and Belgium; and further, French was taught among the rebel soldiers for tactical purposes, and because manuals on the operation of tactical weapons were written in French. A third process, militating in this case against the French policy of preserving Berber tribal and localist loyalties, was one of cultural unification; an Algerian nation was being created by the war. More and more young peasants, for example, began to identify themselves with their wilayats (ALN districts) rather than with language groups or villages.[30]

One question raised in the remarks of the two leaders of the FLN was whether Algeria was being created in the crucible of revolution, or whether the revolution was the result of an already existing Algeria striving for independence. The two members of the FLN implied that both were simultaneously true, that the revolution was making actual a condition that was potential, and which heretofore had found only religious, provincial, and tribalist expression. Without entering into this very complicated logical and sociological question, one might simply ask, was there an Algerian nation by 1961? Over this crucial question, opinions differ widely. The FLN, of course, claimed nearly universal, though oftentimes cowed and intimidated, support from the Moslem population. Many French long denied this. They observed that in the referendum of 1958 96.5 per cent of those who voted gave support to de Gaulle and implicit sanction to the proposition that Algeria is French, and so "saved the Algerians from the dictatorship of a fanatical minority." [31] What seemed probable was that France may have had support (1960) among many peasants that the army was administering in a consciously friendly way, but that the more evolved and dynamic young, the *future*, among the Moslems, were on the side of the FLN. Significant in this connection was what a Moslem administrator said to a reporter of *L'Express* [32] in the autumn of 1960. He stated that he was cooperating with France because of the immediate needs of feeding and ruling his people, and because he hoped that peace might come through the efforts of himself and his colleagues. But the Moslem administrator added: "Without it [the FLN] I wouldn't be here in Paris.[33] All that France has granted us we owe to . . . [the FLN]. The people know this. . . . Understand me, my dear sir, we are all nationalists. This is the truth. But why not take General de Gaulle at his word? One thing is certain. Integration is dead. To be sure, its cadaver still pollutes the atmosphere but our commissions [of *élus*] might contribute to its burial, and help to define Algerian Algeria. But if they [the French] are mocking us it will be terrible. . . . You see, I am sure our way will meet that of the FLN one way or the other. . . ." [34]

The *élu*'s statement was made in 1960 before the myth of fraternization between *colons* and Moslems had perished in the violence of 1961. By the summer of 1961, the evidence to an outside observer seemed conclusive that an Algerian nation had come into being, that it could draw upon the allegiance of the Algerian masses, and that the spokesman of this nation was the FLN. There may have been some truth to de Gaulle's rejection of any parallel between himself in 1940 and Ferhat Abbas in 1960 on the grounds that de Gaulle had not married a German, that he had never in his youth doubted the existence of a French nation, and that he had never favored a German education for his children.[35] But de Gaulle's opinion was becoming rapidly less valid for the younger generation of Algerians, and Abbas, together with his relatively "moderate" colleagues (Ahmed Francis and Abdel Hamid Mehri), fell from power in August 1961.

One consequence of the Algerian war, then, was that by having allowed it to continue for so long, the French lost a cultural capital which they had had over a century to accumulate. The irony was that in fighting to deny the existence of an Algerian soul, if it had not already existed, the French had helped to create one. This nation, Germaine Tillion has written, "we have forged and hardened with our own hands." [36] She reports that in 1955 she witnessed the general disapproval by the people of the Aurès region of Algeria at the assassination of a French instructor, while in 1957 the same people would applaud terroristic assaults upon civilians and children. The terrorists of the FLN by this time, she concluded, had become national heroes.

A second consequence of the war was to make the Moslem youth of Algeria more radical in their plans for the future than they might otherwise have been. This younger generation differs from the generation of Abbas and his colleagues in that it has known France as an enemy only, and in many cases it has not come under the influence of French teachers. Observers have remarked on the degree to which the Moslem Algerian students in the UGEMA became increasingly hostile to any compromise with the French presence. The argument was current in the Algerian trade union, General Union of Algerian Workers (UGTA) in early 1961, that the Algerian revolution was much more than a struggle for independence. It was also an agrarian class war against an exploiting class most of whose members happened to be foreign.[37] And the new president of the GPRA, in August 1961, Ben Youssef Ben Khedda, has never disguised his view that in a sovereign Algeria every trace of "neo-colonialism" should be erased.[38]

In 1943 many of the leaders of the Algerian revolution of 1954 signed the Manifesto of the Algerian People demanding autonomy. One statement made was: "Moslem Algeria does not intend to renounce any part of French and Western culture which remains dear to it. On the contrary, it was in the moral and spiritual wealth of metropolitan France and in the tradition of the liberty of the French people, that it drew the force and the justification for its action today." [39] But the manifesto was composed eleven years before the "Algerian Tragedy" entered its blood-filled denouement.

IX

PROSPECTS — JULY 1962

On July 1 the Algerian people voted overwhelmingly for independence in cooperation with France, and on July 3 President de Gaulle proclaimed the independence of Algeria. But the end of revolution, while it brought exultation to most Algerian Moslems and a sense of relief in metropolitan France, also introduced serious and disturbing problems which had been obscured during the years of revolution. As soon as it became apparent that France, in spite of the clamor and violence of the proponents of "Algérie Française," would be able to fulfill her promise to grant Algerian self-determination, the struggle for leadership in the new Algeria began. This struggle, latent or suppressed while the revolution continued, now emerged to threaten the stability, if not the viability of the new nation. Ahmed Ben Bella, Youssef Ben Khedda, and other veteran leaders of the struggle for independence, were maneuvering for purely personal popularity and power; but also at stake was the future orientation of Algeria. Two issues seemed to be paramount to observers of the North African scene. One was whether Algeria would be dominated by an essentially civilian and democratic government or whether the future government would be heavily mortgaged to the powerful Liberation Army and its commanders. The second issue was whether Algeria would seek to solve its staggering economic problems in alliance with France and the West, or whether it would align itself with Cairo and perhaps with Moscow and Peking. The choices made would have a powerful influence over the future of Tunisia and Morocco and over the role of France in North Africa. But whatever the outcome — and no one could presume to guess this in July 1962 — a part of the new North Africa will be the legacy symbolized in the juxtaposition of the *medina* and the "new city." With the liquidation of French rule in North Africa, France now has the possibility of helping the Arabs to overcome the dichotomy of the two cities. And the independent Arabs of North Africa, who have accused French colonialism of sustaining this dichotomy, may some day admit gratitude that France once created it, and so opened North Africa to the process of modernization.

The stage is now set for the Moslem Arabs to play their own drama in their own fashion. With her fellow Moslems, to quote the Berber poet, Jean Amrouche, the Algerian will now be able ". . . to recover the Algerian heritage buried beneath colonization." [1] But this heritage recovered will never be the same after a century of the French presence. For a time, as in Tunisia and Morocco, the French language, French administrative methods, and French tastes and values will remain an intrinsic part of North African life. The trend, nevertheless, will be toward arabization, toward the recovery of Arabic as bearer of traditional Islamic values, and toward the diminution of the French presence.

The present *évolués* who have led the revolution for national independence, who have used their French education and language to help inspire an anti-French nationalism, have fulfilled a mission. Their children, or the children of their children, might still speak French, but most probably they will write and think in their native Arabic. They will no longer suffer the dilemmas of their fathers or the sense of isolation from their own people that resulted from an alien education.

The prospect for the continuing influence of French culture in the Maghreb, however, is not hopeless. As the director of education in Morocco put it, he would like to see the future Moroccan as a man deeply rooted in Islamic and Arabic culture but at the same time well trained in the French language and in French values. And writers like Malek Haddad have denied that their desire for cultural and linguistic independence is incompatible with their love for French culture. The day may come when the *mission civilisatrice*, shed of its oppressive and colonialist trappings, will leave as legacy only part of itself which is universal and human. Paul Mus once stated that French imperialism offered natives only "the liberty to resemble us." [2] With genuine liberty the children of the *évolués*, freed from the dilemma and cultural unrootedness of their parents, may freely choose to value that part of themselves which remains French. If Germaine Tillion is right, the probability of this being so in Algeria is good. She believed in 1961 that 90 per cent of the Moslems were for the FLN while 60 per cent were in favor of a national development in association with the French. But against Tillion's optimistic guess one could set the pessimism expressed by Pierre-Henri Simon after the Bizerte fiasco and the collapse of the Lugrin negotiations in the summer of 1961. He was now forced to admit that France who has "weaved, in the course of history, the strongest ties of friendship and culture with the Arab peoples . . . is today the power that is the most suspected if not the most detested throughout Islam. . . ." [3] A third observer who has dedicated much effort to preserving the ties of friendship and culture between France and the Arab world, François Mauriac, strikes a balance between hope and despair in his view of the prospects for French culture in North Africa: [4]

> There is an illusion produced by force: the arms we possessed rendered us blind to a virtue proper to France, that of creating free men wherever she has penetrated and wherever she has held dominion — and to create them in spite of the abuse of force. Nothing can alter the fact that French culture produced men like Senghor, Arbousier, Houphouet Boigny. And how rapidly! It needed but one generation. And even in prison, at this very moment, a whole people absorbs our culture. We do violence to the body, but we nourish the spirit.

Assimilation, the policy through which the French once attempted to imprint their culture upon the elite of North Africa is a thing of the past. The leaders of Morocco and Tunisia are attempting to reverse its effects in their new educational policies, and the leaders of Algeria, as well as the intellectuals and writers, have rejected it for their people. But the policy of assimilation has left an imprint which will not be and cannot be eradicated quickly. The French have tended to be two-hearted about the purposes of assimilation: they have considered it both a political weapon and a generous gift. The French-educated leaders of North Africa tend in their turn to be ambivalent about what part to allot to the French language and to French culture in their own liberated cultures. As a weapon of domination they reject the French presence, but as a means of educating their children into the modern world and of remaining in spiritual and intellectual communion with the Western world, they regard this presence as valuable and even necessary. This ambivalence finds reflection in the modern educational systems of Tunisia and Morocco, which remained profoundly bilingual through 1962, and it appears in the contemporary literature which has been produced in Moslem North Africa. Both indicate that while the ideal of assimilation has been rejected in principle and in fact — both Morocco and

Tunisia are committed to progressive arabization — this rejection has not precluded the survival of the French language and of French values in the culture of North Africa. But does the French presence only have this continuity in North Africa because of necessity, because of a lack of teachers and financial resources? Is this presence merely tolerated as an unfortunate and temporary evil? Is it regarded as only a new but subtler form of colonialism? The author's conclusion is that the attitude of the *évolués*, at least, is not this negative. The *évolué* in independence or in revolution against France does sincerely and deeply wish for the continuity of the French cultural presence.[5] But he wishes for this continuity with some serious reservations. Incidents such as Bizerte have made him aware of the danger of depending too heavily upon France for teachers and for subvention. Such a dependence makes Tunisia vulnerable, as was evident on the eve of the beginning of the academic year 1961, when the possibility that France would withdraw her personnel and aid threatened to plunge the educational system of Tunisia into chaos. Incidents such as Bizerte have also made it difficult for the *évolué* to respect and cherish the culture and language of a people who have, in his eyes, insulted or ignored the dignity of his nation. But the importance of the Bizerte incident, or before it of the *Sakiet Sidi Youssef* affair (in 1958) are negligible in their influence compared to the Algerian war.

The cultural effects of the Algerian war can only be surmised. But without doubt the length of the war, the suffering it has caused, and the eruption of the intolerance of the *colons* into savage violence in late 1961 will play their role in influencing relations between France and independent Algeria. In other parts of the world where France has once reigned, the future of the French presence has been significantly influenced by the spirit and the method of French decolonization.

In the Middle East, the manner in which France decolonized (her graceless departure in 1943–45 from Syria and Lebanon,[6] and her dramatic but unfortunate attack upon Egypt in 1956) played no small part in seriously undermining France's cultural and educational influence. In sub-Sahara Africa, on the other hand, the rapidity with which President de Gaulle permitted the states of French-expression to obtain their independence and enter the United Nations, helps to explain why ties of friendship remain strong and French remains the cultural and official language of these states. But in sub-Sahara Africa the elites do not have the same confidence in their traditional cultural heritage as do the Arabs in theirs. Nor do the sub-Sahara Africans have a rich language like Arabic to rely upon as their medium of expression and creativeness.[7] The challenge to France in North Africa is as formidable as the stakes are great. But France still has — even in spite of herself — an opportunity of proving that a cultural amalgam of French and Arabic values is a possibility. The test of such a possibility may well lie in the future of independent Algeria.[8] Looking toward this future, the militants of the FLN, even in revolution, held out hope for a renewal of the French-Moslem dialogue, but for a renewal on a radically different basis from the past. A representative statement in *El-Moudjahid* reads: [9]

The desire to *survive* forces upon the Algerian the need to be himself and also to understand the Other — to assimilate modern experience, but without allowing himself to be assimilated by others.

This double necessity has made the Algerian people both the most nationalistic of peoples and the most open, — both the most faithful to Islam and also the most receptive to extra-islamic values. Of all the Moslem peoples, it is perhaps one of the most faithful to the Moslem faith and at the same time the most deeply imbued with the spirit of the modern West.

Whether yesterday's revolutionary rhetoric can become tomorrow's reality is Algeria's challenge, and also that of France.

SELECTIVE BIBLIOGRAPHY

AND

NOTES

A SELECTIVE BIBLIOGRAPHY

The body of works cited below is limited to sources the author found of particular value to his topic. It is by no means exhaustive. Some titles referred to in the notes are not included here.

Bibliographies

The most useful bibliographies (with comment and description) on responses and reactions of Frenchmen to the North African scene are the two volumes by Aimé Dupuy, *La Tunisie dans les lettres d'expression française* and *L'Algérie dans les lettres d'expression française*, and Roland Lebel, *Le Maroc dans les lettres d'expression française*, all three volumes published in Paris, 1956. A recent and workable bibliography on contemporary research in the field of North African studies is M. Flory *et al.*, "L'Afrique du Nord: état des travaux" in *Revue Française de Science Politique*, 9.2:410–453 (June 1959). A valuable critical bibliography is included in Charles-André Julien, *L'Afrique du Nord en marche: nationalismes musulmans et souveraineté française* (Paris, 1953). Many references appear in the two volumes of René Maunier, trans. E. O. Lorimer, *The Sociology of Colonies: An Introduction to the Study of Race Contact* (London, 1949). On Tunisia, very useful is Paul E. A. Romeril, "Tunisian Nationalism: A Bibliographical Outline" in the *Middle East Journal* (Spring 1960), pp. 206–215.

Periodicals, Newspapers, and Series

Afrique-Action (published weekly in Tunis). With the issue of November 21–27, 1961, the new title is *Jeune Afrique*.

L'Afrique et l'Asie (Paris).

American Universities Field Staff Reports: North Africa Series (the letters of Charles Gallagher are of unusual value).

Annals of the American Academy of Political and Social Science, vols. 298 and 306.

Confluent (Rabat); includes articles on cultural topics.

Encounter (London).

Esprit (Paris); liberal Catholic journal: publishes many articles on North African problems.

Europe-France Outre-mer (Paris); especially the issues of April 1960 on independent Tunisia, and November 1960 on Algeria and the Sahara.

L'Express (Paris); liberal weekly; see especially the articles on contemporary North African issues by Jean Daniel.

IBLA (Revue de l'Institut des Belles Lettres Arabes, Tunis); of particular value on cultural topics; the articles of Michel Lelong are of especial value.

Middle East Journal (Washington, D.C.); includes many articles and book reviews of importance.

Le Monde; the author found this Paris newspaper to be absolutely indispensable on matters involving French North Africa.

Les Temps Modernes (Paris).

New York Times, especially the articles of Thomas Brady.

Que Sais-je? (Presses Universitaires de France); these are small paper-covers by leading authorities who write on a great variety of topics. Useful are Gabriel Esquer, *Histoire d'Algérie* (1951); Georges H. Bousquet, *Les Berbères* (1957); and Pierre Bourdieu, *Sociologie de l'Algérie* (1958).

Tribune Libre (Plon, Paris); has published many documents and controversial essays concerned with North African matters including: Raymond Aron, *La tragédie algérienne* (1957) and *L'Algérie et la république* (1958); Jacques Soustelle, *Le drame algérien et la décadence française* (1957), an attack upon Aron's theses; Roger Stéphane, *La Tunisie de Bourguiba: sept entretiens avec le président de la république tunisienne* (1958); Raymond Jean, *Problèmes d'édification du Maroc et du Maghreb; quatre entretiens avec El Mehdi Ben Barka* (1959); and Charles-Henri Favrod, *La révolution algérienne* (1958) which is rich in quotations from relevant documents and in statistics descriptive of Algerian society in 1954.

Pamphlets and Party Newspapers

Pamphlet material, partly informational and partly propagandistic, is issued by the following:

Ambassade de France: Service de Presse et d'Information (New York).

Front National de Libération (Algeria): their newspaper is *El-Moudjahid* which is published in two editions, one in French and one in Arabic in Tunis.

Union Générale des Etudiants Musulmans Algériens.

Union Générale des Etudiants de Tunisie; their newspaper is *L'Etudiant Tunisien*.

The various political parties of Morocco and Tunisia: the newspaper of the Neo-Destour is *Al-Amal*; the journal of the Moroccan Istiqlal is *Istiqlal*; the journal of the Union Nationale des Forces Populaires (in French) is *L'Avant-garde*. Of considerable value is the abundant material issued by the Secrétariat d'Etat à l'Information (now called Information et Culture) of Tunisia. See their handsomely published "La Tunisie au travail," in particular, which is richly illustrated and includes useful statistical diagrams. Also published are almost all of the speeches made by President Bourguiba. Of value is the mimeographed tri-weekly *La Documentation Tunisienne*.

Material on education is published by the Ministère de l'Education Nationale (Morocco) and the Secrétariat d'Etat à l'Education Nationale (Tunisia). See especially: *Le mouvement éducatif au Maroc durant l'année scolaire 1959–1960*, and *Nouvelle conception de l'enseignement en Tunisie (1958–1959)*.

Studies of a General and Comprehensive Nature

Barbour, Nevill, *A Survey of North West Africa (The Maghrib)*, London, 1959. This is the most valuable single volume study of North Africa in English.

Berque, Jacques, *Le Maghreb entre deux guerres*, Paris, 1962. A comprehensive sociological study by a brilliant ethnologist.

Bonn, Gisela, *Neue Welt am Atlas: was geht vor in Marokko, Algerien, Tunesien?*, Wiesbaden, 1955. Popular, but with illuminating insights into aspects of North Africa on the eve of Tunisian and Moroccan independence..

Brunschwig, Henry, *La colonisation française du pacte colonial à l'union française*, Paris, 1949. A reliable general guide.

Deschamps, Hubert, *Les méthodes et les doctrines coloniales de la France du xvi⁰ siècle à nos jours*, Paris, 1953. A reliable and most useful survey of the ideas behind French imperialism.

————,*The French Union: History, Institutions, Economy, Countries and Peoples, Social and Political Changes*, Paris, 1956.

Devèze, Michel, *La France d'outre-mer: de l'empire colonial à l'union française, 1938–1947*, Paris, 1948.

Emerson, Rupert, *From Empire to Nation: The Rise to Self-Assertion of Asian and African Peoples*, Cambridge, Mass., 1960.

Fanon, Frantz, *Les damnés de la terre*, Paris, 1961.

al-Fassi, Allal, trans., H. Z. Nuseibeh, *The Independence Movements in Arab North Africa*, Washington, D.C., 1954.

Furniss, Edgar S., Jr., *France, Troubled Ally*, New York, 1960. The first section outlines the interaction between French domestic and colonial history.

Hahn, Lorna, *North Africa, Nationalism to Nationhood*, Washington, D.C., 1960. Comprehensive but not free from slips and errors.

Hanotaux, Gabriel and Alfred Martineau, eds., *Histoire des colonies françaises et de l'expansion de la France dans le monde*. In Volume II is Augustin Bernard, "L'Algérie" (Paris, 1930) and Volume III contains Georges Hardy, "Le Maroc-La Tunisie" (Paris, 1931). Both Hardy and Bernard are scholarly but are prejudiced in favor of the French mission and accomplishment.

Hardy, Georges, *Histoire de la colonisation française*, Paris, 1928.

Julien, Charles-André, *L'Afrique du Nord en marche: nationalismes musulmans et souveraineté française*, Paris, 1953. The best one-volume study known to the present author of the modern history of French North Africa. The author is a distinguished historian with sympathy for North African nationalism.

Lacouture Jean, *Cinq hommes et la France*, Paris, 1961.

Luethy, Herbert, trans. E. Mosbacher, *France against Herself*, New York, 1955. Satiric, clever, but sometimes exaggerated.

Monteil, Vincent, *L'arabe moderne*, Paris, 1960.

Mumford, William Bryant and Major G. St.J. Orde-Brown, *Africans Learn to be French*, London, [1937?].

Murphy, Agnes, *The Ideology of French Imperialism; 1871–1881*, Washington, D.C., 1948.

Mus, Paul, *Le destin de l'union française de l'Indochine à l'Afrique*, Paris, 1954. Searching, philosophical, difficult.

Park, Julian, ed., *The Culture of France in our Time*, Ithaca, 1954.

Priestley, Herbert I., *France Overseas: A Study of Modern Imperialism*, New York, London, 1938.

Roberts, Stephen H., *History of French Colonial Policy (1870–1925)*, 2 vols., London, 1929. Comprehensive, critical, sometimes tendentious, but a valuable antidote to works by Frenchmen.

Schuman, Frederick L., *War and Diplomacy in the French Republic*, New York, London, 1931. An illuminating study of French imperialism as a part of general French political strategy.

Walker, Eric A., *Colonies*, Cambridge, Eng., 1944. A suggestive comparative essay on colonialism.

Werth, Alexander, *The Strange History of Pierre Mendès-France and the Great Conflict over French North Africa*, London, 1957. Some of the same material is contained in Werth's *France 1940–55*, London, 1956.

Studies of Particular Topics

Abbas, Ferhat, *Le jeune algérien*, Paris, 1931.

Ardant, Gabriel, *La Tunisie d'aujourd'hui et de demain*, Paris, 1961.

Ashford, Douglas E., *Political Change in Morocco*, Princeton, 1961.

Balafrej, Ahmed, "Morocco Plans for Independence," *Foreign Affairs*, 34.3:483–489 (April 1956).

Behr, Edward, *The Algerian Problem*, London, 1961.

Bennabi, Malek, *Vocation de l'Islam*, Paris, 1954.

Betts, Raymond, *Assimilation and Association in French Colonial Theory, 1890–1914*, New York, London, 1961.

Bloch-Michel, Jean, trans. R. Howard, "Paris Letter," *Partisan Review* (Winter 1959), pp. 95–99.

Bouderbala, N. "Camus parmi nous," *Education Nationale* (Rabat), January 3, 1960, pp. 65–69.

Bourguiba, Habib, *La Tunisie et la France: vingt-cinq ans de lutte pour une coopération libre*, Paris, 1954.

Brace, Richard and Joan, *Ordeal in Algeria*, Princeton, 1960.

Bromberger, Serge, *Les rebelles algériens*, Paris, 1958.

Brown, L. C., "Tunis under the French Protectorate: A History of Ideological Change," unpublished doctoral dissertation, Harvard University, 1962. A very helpful consideration of the process of modernization in Tunisia. Brown is also author of letters issued by the Institute of Current World Affairs (New York). Useful in the present context are: "Tunisia: Education, 'Cultural Unity' and the Future" (December 1, 1960) and "Colonization — A Second Look" (May 23, 1961).

Brunschvig, Robert and Gustave E. Grunebaum, eds., *Classicisme et déclin culturel dans l'histoire de l'Islam*, Paris, 1957. Of especial value is the article by Brunschvig, "Problèmes de la décadence," pp. 29–46.

Catroux, Georges, *Lyautey, le marocain*, Paris, 1952.

———, *Dans la bataille de Méditerranée: Egypte, Levant, Afrique du Nord, 1940–1944*, Paris, 1949.

Chatelain, Yves, *La vie littéraire et intellectuelle en Tunisie de 1900 à 1937*, Paris, 1937.

Clark, Michael, *Algeria in Turmoil: A History of the Rebellion*, New York, 1959. To be read with caution because of its definite pro-*colon* bias.

Demeerseman, André, *Tunisie: sève nouvelle*, Paris, 1957.

Fanon, Frantz, *L'an V de la révolution algérienne*, Paris, 1959.

Garas, Felix, *Bourguiba et la naissance d'une nation*, Paris, 1956.

Grandval, Gilbert, *Ma mission au Maroc*, Paris, 1956.

Halstead, John P., "The Origins of Moroccan Nationalism 1919–1934," unpublished doctoral dissertation, Harvard University, 1960. Contains material on the nature and influence of French education under the Protectorate.

Hanotaux, Gabriel, *et al.*, *L'empire colonial français*, Paris, 1929. Includes essays by French colonialists rationalizing and praising the French venture.

Hardy, Georges, "L'éducation français au Maroc," *La Revue de Paris* (April 1921), pp. 773–788.

Jeanson, Colette and Francis, *L'Algérie hors la loi*, Paris, 1955. A leftist work that is a valuable antidote to Clark's book, and vice versa.

Julien, Charles-André, "France and Islam," *Foreign Affairs* (July 1940), pp. 680–699.

———, "Jules Ferry" in *Les politiques d'expansion impérialiste*, ed. P. Renouvin, Paris, 1949.

Khairallah, Chedly, "Le mouvement jeune tunisien," vol. I of *Essai d'histoire et de synthèse des mouvements nationalistes tunisiens*, Tunis, n.d.

Lacouture, Jean and Simonne, *Le Maroc à l'épreuve*, Paris, 1958.

Laitman, Leon, *Tunisia Today: Crisis in North Africa*, New York, 1954.

Landau, Rom, *Moroccan Drama 1900–1955*, London, 1956.

———, *Morocco Independent: Under Mohammed the Fifth*, London, 1961.

———, *Moroccan Journal*, London, 1952.

———, *The Sultan of Morocco*, London, 1951.

de Latour, P. Boyer, *Vérités sur l'Afrique du Nord*, Paris 1956. A colonialist point of view.

Lelong, Michel, "Culture arabe et culture occidentale dans la Tunisie d'aujourd'hui" (Une enquête de la revue *Al-Fikr*), *IBLA*, 19:313–331 (1956).

Leroy-Beaulieu, Paul, *L'Algérie et la Tunisie*, Paris, 1897.

Le Tourneau, Roger, *Evolution politique de l'Afrique du Nord musulman 1920–1961*, Paris, 1962. The most useful general political survey available. The last chapter is a particularly interesting discussion of the problems and prospects of Maghreb unity.

———, "North Africa: Rigorism and Bewilderment" in *Unity and Variety in Muslim Civilization*, ed., G. E. von Grunebaum, Chicago, 1955.

Mandouze, André, *La révolution algérienne par les textes*, Paris, 1961.

Memmi, Albert, *Portrait du colonisé, précédé du portrait du colonisateur*, Paris, 1957.

Montagne, Robert, *Révolution au Maroc*, Paris, 1952.

de Montéty, *Femmes de Tunisie*, Paris, 1958. A more comprehensive study of modernization in Tunisia than the title would indicate.

de Montvalon, Robert, *Ces pays qu'on n'appellera plus colonies*, Paris, 1956.

For another work representing the liberal Catholic point of view, see Robert Barrat, *Justice pour le Maroc*, Paris, 1953, with preface by François Mauriac.

Nora, Pierre, *Les français d'Algérie*, Paris, 1961.

La Nouvelle Critique, issue of January, 1960, which is devoted to a study by various intellectuals of the problems of Algerian culture. Among the most useful articles are those by Dr. Sadek Hadjeres and Abdalhaq Annaciri.

Power, Thomas F., Jr., *Jules Ferry and the Renaissance of French Imperialism*, New York, 1944.

Raymond, André, *La Tunisie*, Paris, 1961.

Rézette, Robert, *Les partis politiques marocains*, Paris, 1955. Is still useful especially in regard to the cultural setting in which Moroccan political life functions.

Rivlin, Benjamin, "Cultural Conflicts in French North Africa," *Annals of the American Academy of Political and Social Science*, 306:4–9 (July 1956).

Roy, Jules, *Autour du drame*, Paris, 1961.

———, *La guerre d'Algérie*, Paris, 1960.

Sarrasin, Paul Emile, *La crise algérienne*, Paris, 1949. Includes useful excerpts from documents.

Sebag, Paul, *La Tunisie*, Paris, 1951.

Soustelle, Jacques, *Aimée et souffrante Algérie*, Paris, 1956.

Taillard, Fulbert, *Le nationalisme marocain*, Paris, 1947. Includes useful excerpts from documents.

Tillion, Germaine, trans., R. Matthews, *Algeria: The Realities*, New York, 1959.

———, *Les ennemis complémentaires*, Paris, 1960. This has been translated into English by R. Howard as *France and Algeria: Complementary Enemies*, New York, 1961.

Tlatli, Salah-Eddine, *Tunisie nouvelle: problèmes et perspectives*, Tunis, 1957.

de Tocqueville, Alexis, "Notes du voyage en Algérie de 1841" in *Oeuvres, papiers et correspondances*, ed., J.-P. Mayer, vol. V:2, Paris, 1952.

Toynbee, Arnold J., *Survey of International Affairs 1937*, 2 vols., London, 1938. Toynbee discusses the Blum-Viollette Bill at length in vol. I, pp. 486–543.

Viollette, Maurice, *L'Algérie vivra-t-elle?: notes d'un ancien gouverneur général*, Paris, 1931. Defends the principle of his future bill.

Literary Works

The novels referred to in the text are all readily available, as are the works of Albert Camus. Most of the works of the North African writers have been published by the Editions du Seuil (Paris) and by René Julliard (Paris). Almost all of Camus' works are published by Gallimard (Paris: NRF).

Works that received particular attention in the text of the present book are:

Chraibi, Driss, *Le passé simple*, Paris, 1955.

Dib, Mohammed, *La grande maison*, Paris, 1952.
———, *L'incendie*, Paris, 1954.
Feraoun, Mouloud, *La terre et le sang*, Paris, 1953.
Haddad, Malek, *L'élève et la leçon*, Paris, 1960.
Mammeri, Mouloud, *Le sommeil du juste*. Translated into English by L. Ortzen as *The Sleep of the Just*, Boston, n.d.
Memmi, Albert, *La statue de sel*. Translated into English by E. Roditi as *The Pillar of Salt*, London, 1956.
Yacine, Kateb, *Nedjma*, Paris, 1956.
———, *Le cercle de représailles*, Paris, 1959.

The works of Albert Camus that are particularly relevant to the themes of the present book are:

Actuelles, III, Paris, 1958. The subtitle is "Chronique algérienne."
L'envers et l'endroit, Paris, 1958.
L'été, Paris, 1954.
L'étranger, Paris, 1942.
L'exil et le royaume: nouvelles, Paris, 1957.
L'homme révolté, Paris, 1951.
Les justes, Paris, 1950.

NOTES

CHAPTER I: INTRODUCTION

1. *Les damnés de la terre* (Paris, 1961). Fanon, a French-trained psychiatrist born in Martinique, came to identify himself with the Algerian nation in revolution and during his last years referred to himself as an Algerian. Translations, unless otherwise specified, are those of the present author.

2. Littré's *Dictionnaire de la langue française* (1885) defines *évolué* in the following way: "terme didactique. Qui a subi son évolution, son développement."

3. Of the two cities, Fanon writes with bitterness: "The city of the *colon* is a city of white men, of strangers. . . . The city of the colonized, or at least the native city, the negro village, the *medina*, the reservation, is a place of ill-repute, peopled by men of ill-repute. . . . The colonial world is a manichaean world." *Les damnés de la terre*, pp. 32–33.

The word *colon* will be used in the present monograph to designate all French settlers in North Africa, both rural and urban.

CHAPTER II: THE MISSION CIVILISATRICE

1. William Bryant Mumford and Major G. St.J. Orde-Brown, *Africans Learn to be French* (London, [1937?]), p. 89.

2. "The Ancient Jar of Dahomey," *Encounter* (September 1959), pp. 33–39. See also V. Thompson and R. Adloff, *French West Africa* (Stanford, 1957), pp. 190 ff. for a discussion of the irony of native *évolués* desiring the revival of cultures in which they have no confidence. John Gunther, in *Inside Africa* (London, 1955), chap. xxxiv, describes how predisposed Black Africans are to assimilation to French culture.

3. Harold Nicolson in *Diplomacy* (London, 1939), pp. 150–153, makes the following observation:
"The French combine with acuteness of observation a special gift of lucid persuasiveness. They are honourable and precise. Yet they lack tolerance. So convinced is the average Frenchman of his own intellectual pre-eminence, so conscious is he of the superiority of his own culture, that he finds it difficult at times to conceal his impatience with the barbarians who inhabit other countries. This causes offense. . . . Moreover, their passion for logic, the legal temper of their minds, their extreme realism, their distrust of all political emotion, often blind them to the motives, the feelings and often the

thoughts of other nations. Their superb intellectual integrity tempts them to regard as insincere the confused fumblings of less lucid minds and to feel irritated, dry contempt, when what is necessary is a little lucubrating indulgence. It thus occurs that French diplomacy, with all its magnificent equipment and its fine principles, is often ineffective."

4. Cited in Mumford and Orde-Brown, *Africans Learn to be French*, p. 50.

5. See V. Mallinson, *An Introduction to the Study of Comparative Education* (Melbourne, 1957); J. Park, "Education" in *The Culture of France in our Time*, ed. J. Park (Ithaca, 1954), pp. 194–223; E. S. Furniss, Jr., *France: Troubled Ally* (New York, 1960), pp. 141–145, 420–422; a summary of the proposed reforms of the Comité Reuff-Armand in *Le Monde*, September 22, 1960, p. 8. Full of insights is J. G. Weightman's "The Sorbonne," *Encounter* (June 1961), pp. 28–42. A useful study of the application of the French educational system abroad is Mumford and Orde-Brown, *Africans Learn to be French*.

For a recent general critical account of French education, see A. Kerr, *Schools of Europe* (London, 1961), chap. vi. A French educational authority, Marcel Hignette, describes the French system of education as one that emphasizes intellect, theory, and humanistic values. He describes the French system as "Cartesian" and states that for Frenchmen "culture is above all literary." "The Primacy of the Rational in French Secondary Education" in *The Year Book of Education 1958* (London, 1959), pp. 233–241.

6. This statement appears in Habib Kurani, "Evolution in Education" in *Evolution in the Middle East: Reform, Revolt and Change*, ed. S. N. Fisher (Washington, D.C., 1953), pp. 3–12, 8. Kurani writes from the point of view of an educationalist trained in the American system of education.

7. *Journal des Débats*, March 19, 1883. French views of Moslem decadence are discussed by R. Brunschvig, "Problèmes de la décadence" in *Classicisme et déclin culturel dans l'histoire de l'Islam*, eds. R. Brunschvig and G. E. von Grunebaum (Paris, 1957), pp. 29–46.

8. Georges Hardy in *L'empire colonial français*, Gabriel Hanotaux et al. (Paris, 1929), p. 346, 357–358.

9. J. Trimingham, *Islam in West Africa* (Oxford, 1959), pp. 209 ff.

10. A prominent contemporary French educator quoted in Charles-André Julien, *Afrique du Nord en marche: nationalismes musulmans et souveraineté française* (Paris, 1953), pp. 36–37. See also statements in this spirit made by leading French educators at the Congress of the French Language in the Countries of the Mediterranean (July 16–20, 1922) published in *Notre langue dans le bassin de la Méditerranée* (Paris, 1923).

11. George Kirk, *The Middle East in the War*, Survey of International Affairs 1939–1946 (London, 1952), p. 305, fn. 1. And Ignace Lepp in *Midi sonne au Maroc* (quoted in Rom Landau, *Moroccan Drama: 1900–1955*, (London, 1956) concluded: "It would be dishonest to describe the Moroccan

nationalists as our enemies, as is being done nowadays by Frenchmen in
Morocco and by the metropolitan papers that support them. . . . Without
any doubt, the nationalist elite is closest to ourselves, both intellectually and
morally. . . . Suspicious of both (native) youth and intellectuals, the French
Administration treated the growing nationalism with a sovereign dis-
dain. . . . Held in contempt and persecuted by the French, the nationalists
became anti-French and xenophone (sic). Whose fault was it? Too weak to
fight alone, they were bound to turn towards the Arab east." Moroccan
évolués were denied any real participation in the administration of their
country, and the French, according to Landau, *Moroccan Drama*, pp. 56,
147, 168, 170, refused to take the political demands of the proto-nationalists
seriously.

12. *Ma mission au Maroc* (Paris, 1956), p. 21.

13. *France Against Herself*, trans. E. Mosbacher (New York, 1955), p. 217.
Perhaps the last responsible gasp of this presumption was the statement made
in 1958 by Prime Minister Michel Debré that every person "from Dunkirk
to Tamanrasset" was a Frenchman.

14. P. Leroy-Beaulieu, *L'Algérie et la Tunisie* (Paris, 1887), pp. 251–252,
274–275.

15. A. Bernard, "L'Algérie" in *Histoire des colonies françaises et de
l'expansion de la France dans le monde*, eds. G. Hanotaux and A. Martineau
(Paris, 1930), p. 534.

16. These quotations are taken from D. de Rougement, "Le nationalisme
et l'Europe" in *La Table Ronde* (March 1960), pp. 9–26.

17. Hubert Deschamps, *Les méthodes et doctrines coloniales de la France
du xvie siècle à nos jours* (Paris, 1953), p. 11; Felix Garas, *Bourguiba et la
naissance d'une nation* (Paris, 1956), p. 7; Julien, *L'Afrique du Nord en
marche*, p. 53; Henry Brunschwig, *La colonisation française: du pacte coloniale à l'union française* (Paris, 1949), p. 265. Charles-Henri Favrod suggests
that Frenchmen tend to believe that their colonialism must be progressive
since it was France that gave the world the modern institutions and language of liberty during the French Revolution. He cites Jules Michelet as
having had insight into the French proselytizing tendency in the nineteenth
century when "France sought to impose upon the vanquished her own personality, not as her own, but as the model of the good and the beautiful."
L'Afrique seule (Paris, 1961), pp. 17 and 27.

18. R. Maunier, *The Sociology of Colonies: An Introduction to the Study
of Race Contact*, trans. E. O. Lorimer; 2 vols. (London, 1949), vol. I, p. 42.

19. Robert Montagne, *Révolution au Maroc* (Paris, 1952), 148. For a discussion of the eventual failure of Lyautey's system, see General Catroux,
Lyautey, le Marocain (Paris, 1952).

20. J. Cady, *The Roots of French Imperialism in Eastern Asia* (Ithaca,
1954), pp. 295–296.

21. Jules Harmand, a diplomat and colonial administrator just before the
turn of the century, and the author of the influential book *Domination et*

colonisation (Paris, 1910), was the first important colonialist to advocate the compromise with the policy of assimilation that "association" represents. See Deschamps, *Les méthodes et les doctrines coloniales de la France*, p. 150. There have been French theorists of colonialism who have repudiated the idea of assimilation completely. Gustave Le Bon, for example, denied the possibility of assimilation because, he argued, each people has its own laws of development, its own characteristics which are deeper than the similarities between men made so much of during the Enlightenment. His disciple, Léopold de Saussure, once wrote: "If one imposes on one race the institutions conceived for another, one produces disorder, anarchy or despotism." See Deschamps, p. 146. Some French colonialists have also argued that cultural assimilation should only be offered to non-French European settlers in French colonies. Hardy, for example, once maintained that it was dangerous to educate non-European natives who might some day turn their knowledge against metropolitan France. See "L'éducation française au Maroc" in *La Revue de Paris*, 12.2, 773–788 (April 1921). But it has been the policy advocated by Harmand that has prevailed and been the characteristic French policy in regard to cultural expansion. A useful survey discussion of the role of the theories of Assimilation and Association in French colonial policy before World War I is R. Betts, *Assimilation and Association in French Colonial Theory 1890–1914* (New York, London, 1961).

22. *Colonies* (Cambridge, Eng., 1944), pp. 101–102.

23. *Le Monde* (weekly), *571* (September 1959), p. 1.

24. *Ibid.*, *561* (July 1959), p. 4.

25. *Ibid.*, *528* (December 1958). The article is by Jacqueline Piatier.

26. About 20,000 French teachers worked outside of French territories in 1960, and more were needed. According to *Le Monde*, *625* (October 1960), p. 8, France exports more teachers than any other nation in the world. In 1961 the number of foreign students studying in France was second largest in the world after the United States. See *Time*, September 8, 1961, p. 46. In 1961–62 there were 32,000 foreign students in the Faculties. This was 13 per cent of the total 237,000. See *Le Monde*, October 17, 1961, p. 16.

27. In some cases, names will be transliterated in this monograph as they appear in the French press and in French books. Such transliterations are not always consistent with others used in this study.

28. *Le Monde*, *564* (August 1959), p. 3. This article is part of a series entitled "Le Maroc, monarchie populaire" which begins with no. *563*. Roger Vaurs in "The Role of France and the French in Northern Africa" in *The Annals* 306:17–25 (July 1956), observes that in 1956 the Moroccan cabinet included thirteen ministers with higher degrees from France.

29. *From Empire to Nation: The Rise to Self-Assertion of Asian and African Peoples* (Cambridge, Mass., 1960), p. 209. Fanon, as indicated in a previous chapter, believes that "the nationalists of the Western school" will and should lose the allegiance of the masses.

CHAPTER III: THE FRENCH PRESENCE SIX YEARS AFTER INDEPENDENCE:
TUNISIA AND MOROCCO

1. At the Belgrade Conference on September 6, 1961. See *New York Times* (International), September 7, 1961, pp. 1, 3. The relationship between Morocco and France was temporarily shaken in the month of November, 1961, when the Algerian prisoners, Ben Bella and his companions, embarked upon their hunger strike. The Moroccan government, because of popular pressure and because the five Algerian rebels had been captured in 1956 while guests of the king of Morocco, felt compelled to insist strongly to the French that the status of the prisoners be changed. A final compromise made toward the end of November gave the Moroccan government the right to provide the prisoners with Moroccan doctors and to maintain political liaison with them. Hassan II, of course, was obliged, in order to retain power, to do all that was possible to aid and abet the Algerian movement and to pay at least lip service to the ideal of Maghreb unity. In January 1962, the FLN and the Moroccan government established a commission on a ministerial level to consider a "United Arab Maghreb" and to draft a North African Charter.

2. *Le Monde*, July 26, 1960, p. 9.

3. *Le Monde*, *450*, (November 1957), p. 3.

4. The Moroccan was the largest French Cultural and University Mission in the world in 1960–61. Also important in dispensing a French education in Morocco, among the Jewish population, has been the Alliance Israélite Universelle. In 1956 it supported 75 schools in Morocco which served 29,345 students. See G. Ollivier, *L'alliance israélite universelle: 1860–1960* (Paris, 1959), p. 212. In Tunisia, in 1956, there were five Alliance schools with 3,607 students.

5. Nevill Barbour, *A Survey of North West Africa* (London, 1959), pp. 118–119.

6. *Europe-France Outre-mer* (March 1961), pp. 61–62.

7. Rom Landau, *Morocco Independent: Under Mohammed the Fifth* (London, 1961), pp. 14, 78, and 139. One hectare is 2.47 acres. According to the *New York Herald Tribune* (Paris edition), January 13–14, 1962, 10,000 French experts remained in Morocco (in early 1962). Of these, 8,600 were teachers and the Moroccan government was asking for 500 additional French teachers.

8. *Enseigner en Tunisie, 1960*, issued by the *Direction Générale des Affaires Culturelles et Techniques du Ministère des Affaires Etrangères*.

9. *La Documentation Tunisienne*, June 25, 1958.

10. *Le Monde*, *680* (August 1961), p. 2. The figures cited in *Afrique-Action*, August 14, 1961, p. 13, are somewhat different but both sets of figures referred to add up to around 3,000 French teachers serving in all branches of education in Tunisia. Excluding the Cultural Mission, *Afrique-Action* indicates there were 1,457 French teachers (in 1961) from among

a total of 9,313 teachers in all branches of Tunisian education. The director of the French Cultural Mission could boast that after four years of the complete primary cycle, beginning in October 1958, Tunisian students would have spent more time studying French than Arabic, *Le Monde*, August 9, 1958. Cited in Vincent Monteil, *L'arabe moderne* (Paris, 1960), p. 99.

In 1961, the number of Tunisian students studying in France was 1,250. The next largest representation was in Lebanon with 84. In other French-speaking countries the representation was 290 (Switzerland and Belgium); in Arab countries (Iraq and the U.A.R.) the number was 77, and in communist lands the number was 13 (Soviet Russia and Yugoslavia). See *Afrique-Action*, September 2–8, 1961, p. 16.

11. El-Gabsi in *Afrique-Action*, July 31, 1961, pp. 6–7. For another summary of French assets in Tunisia in July, 1961, see *Le Monde, 666* (July 1961), p. 3.

12. These figures were supplied by the Tunisian Ministry of Information. It should be noted that these figures are influenced by the fact of the greater prosperity of readers in French, of subsidies, of the number of times a single copy in Arabic may change hands. Subscriptions are not included, and the figures are approximate. Some of the figures on circulation in 1957 were as follows: the two Arabic papers sold 30,000 copies; *La Dépêche*, the French *colon* paper, 25,000; the destourian *Le Petit Matin* and *La Presse* together sold 30,000. The weekly *L'Action* sold 1,700. See Michel Lelong, "La vie intellectuelle et artistique en Tunisie," *IBLA* 20:239–268 (1957).

13. A brief item in *Jeune Afrique*, December 27, 1961–January 2, 1962, p. 17, indicates that the figures had not appreciably changed for the year 1961.

14. *La Presse* (Tunis), July 29, 1960, p. 1. According to the *New York Herald Tribune* (Paris edition), January 13–14, 1962, 150,000 *colons* still remained in Morocco in early 1962. André Raymond, in *La Tunisie* (Paris, 1961), pp. 50–51, states that in 1961 there were still as many as 80–90,000 French in Tunisia out of 130,000 Europeans.

15. See Rom Landau, *Moroccan Journal* (London, 1952) and Fulbert Taillard, *Le nationalisme marocain* (Paris, 1947), pp. 100 ff. The second presents a *colon* point of view.

A revealing illustration of the arrogant short-sightedness of many Moroccan *colons* appears in the remarks of Boniface, prefect of Casablanca, to Alexander Werth in April, 1953. Boniface dismissed the Istiqlal, for example, as ". . . a few half-baked intellectuals with wishy-washy ideas about Western democracy and the French Revolution. The Moroccan people despise them. . . ." Alexander Werth, *France 1940–55* (New York, 1956), pp. 619–620.

16. One might observe that up through 1961 the Moroccan *colons* were tolerated in spite of the memory of scenes of violence, before and after liberation. In December 1952, several hundred Arab demonstrators were killed in Casablanca (after the assassination of the Tunisian labor leader

Ferhat Hached), and on October 23, 1956, following the capture by the French of Ben Bella and his companions, fifty Frenchmen were massacred in Meknes and environs. This is to point only to the spontaneous violence that has been possible in Morocco between the two communities without mention of the thousands killed during the struggle between French forces and the Liberation Army.

17. For a useful comparison of politics in Tunisia and Morocco, see Douglas Ashford, "Transitional Politics in Morocco and Tunisia" in *Current Problems in North Africa* (Princeton, 1959), pp. 14–35. André Demeerseman's statement appears in *Tunisie: sève nouvelle* (Paris, 1957). Bourguiba declared in 1957 in an article in *Foreign Affairs* (July 1957), pp. 646–653: "As for Tunisia, it has chosen unequivocally to follow the free world of the West." And ". . . because it is situated in the 'West', and is neighbor to Europe and particularly to France, it looks for security and economic progress to a close alliance with the free nations of the West." A Tunisian journalist once told the author: "Our answer to the cliché which says that Morocco is the lion, Algeria the man, while Tunisia is the woman of North Africa, is, look at the results."

18. For a detailed discussion of the French presence in Tunisia, see *Europe-France Outre-mer* (April 1960). This is a special issue devoted to Tunisia after four years of independence.

19. *L'Express*, July 27, 1961, pp. 3–6. The Tunisian government claimed that 1,300 Tunisians were killed compared to 30 French soldiers. Another estimate, by Red Cross observers, was that 5–6,000 Tunisians were killed. See *L'Express*, October 12, 1961, p. 13.

20. *L'Express*, August 24, 1961, p. 3, and July 27, p. 33. *Time*, July 28, 1961, pp. 20–21.

21. Bechir Ben Yahmed, *Afrique-Action*, July 24 and August 7, 1961. J. Lacouture, *Le Monde*, August 8, 1961, p. 7. Masmoudi was the Minister of Information until October 1961. A saying in the Middle East in the summer of 1961 was "Bourguibism is dead, but Bourguiba lives. Ben Youssef is dead, but Youssefism lives." Salah Ben Youssef was assassinated in August 1961 in Germany. He had been Bourguiba's most bitter Tunisian opponent and had identified himself with Nasserism.

22. Between July 20 and October 15, 1961, 7,860 French citizens were repatriated from Tunisia. More were expected to return. *Le Monde*, October 15–16, 1961, p. 5.

23. After Bourguiba had concluded that he would have to compromise with the French over Bizerte, there remained the problem for both the Tunisian government and France of persuading the French Rightists and the young Tunisian militants to accept this compromise. See Henri de Montéty, "Responsables français et tunisiens devront convaincre les ultras et les 'Jeunes Turcs'" in *Le Monde*, October 3, 1961, pp. 1, 3.

24. See Landau, *Morocco Independent*, pp. 88–89.

25. See Chapter VIII.

CHAPTER IV: ALGERIAN COLONS AND THE CRISIS OF THE FRENCH PRESENCE

1. Pierre Nora in *Les français d'Algérie* (Paris, 1961), pp. 232–233, states that the French *colon* population is probably not much more than 800,000. In addition there are 150,000 Jews, a community with its own personality, and about 60,000 unnaturalized Spanish and Italians. The figure Algerian *colons* cite for their population, 1,200,000, is therefore considerably exaggerated. A useful study of Algerian demography is Dorothy Good, "Notes on the Demography of Algeria" in *Population Index* (January 1961), pp. 3–32.

2. A dramatic picture of *colon* domination of Algeria as well as of Tunisia and Morocco before independence appears in Claude Bourdet, "Les maîtres de l'Afrique du Nord" in *Les Temps Modernes* (June 1952), pp. 2254–2264.

3. Julien, *L'Afrique du Nord en marche*, pp. 27–29.

4. *The Listener*, February 18, 1960. See the series by Jules Roy beginning in *L'Express*, September 29, 1960, for an insight into how racialist the *colons* really are. These articles have appeared in book form as *La guerre d'Algérie* (Paris, 1960). Roy is of Algerian *colon* origin. The fullest study of the Algerian *colons* is Nora's *Les français d'Algérie*. Henri Kréa's novel, *Djemal*, (1961), is a bitter and searching indictment of the racialism of the *colons*. The hero (Kréa himself?) is the son of a French-Arab marriage. The experience of discrimination leads him to join the rebellion against France.

5. Alexis de Tocqueville, "Notes du voyage en Algérie de 1841" in *Oeuvres, papiers et correspondances*, ed. J.-P. Mayer (Paris, 1952), vol. V:2, pp. 216–217.

6. Nora observes that the myth-makers of the Algerian *colons*, Louis Bertrand and Robert Rondau, tried to argue that the "soul" of Algeria was not Islamic at all. Bertrand believed it to be Greco-Roman and Rondau saw it as a new synthesis in the making with French the dominant ingredient. Bertrand ignored Islam, while Rondau saw it as an obstacle to the birth of the new Algeria. Nora, *Les français d'Algérie*, pp. 144 ff.

7. Roy, *La guerre d'Algérie* and Nora, *Les français d'Algérie*.

8. *Le jeune algérien* (Paris, 1931), pp. 102, 117, 128.

9. Jean Pelegri stated that he had come to the same conclusions as Jules Roy about the tragic futility of the Algerian war. After reading Roy's *La guerre d'Algérie*, he asked in a letter to *L'Express*, November 10, 1961: "How can one fail to see that the war debases [*dénature*] everything. . .?" Pierre Popie, a liberal lawyer, believed French and Arabs could live together in an independent Algeria. He provided legal counsel to captured Algerian rebels. He was assassinated in 1961, probably by *colon* "ultras." Jean Daniel, born in Algeria of Jewish parents, covered the North African scene for *L'Express* until he was wounded during the Bizerte affair.

10. Magazine of the *New York Times*, July 21. The liberal mayor of G. . ., discussed on p. 26, had a bomb thrown at his house by French

"ultras" in the summer of 1960. By the autumn of 1961 the terrorism liberal *colons* were subjected to reached a climax. By this time the ultra Secret Army Organization controlled much of the life of the Algerian cities, and liberals felt abandoned by metropolitan France. See *Afrique-Action*, October 14–20, 1961, pp. 6–8.

11. Raymond Aron in an article in *Preuves* (October 1961), cited in *Le Monde*, October 25, 1961, p. 6.

12. In *L'Express*, September 28, 1961, p. 25.

13. See E. Mannoni's description of the hotbed of terror Oran had become by the end of the summer of 1961 in *Le Monde*, September 5, 1961, pp. 1, 7. Between January 1 and October, 1961, 100,000 *colons* had emigrated from Algeria. See *L'Express*, October 12, 1961, p. 9. And during the year from December, 1960 to December, 1961, 40,000 Europeans had left the region of Oran. In the winter of 1961, 2,000 were leaving each month. See *Le Monde*, December 10–11, p. 6. The *New York Herald Tribune* (Paris edition), January 13–14, 1962, described the scene in Oran in the following way: "A virtually powerless French administration infiltrated by agents of Rightist terrorists pleads for help and prays for a miracle in this, Algeria's second metropolis. . . . Oran, a city of 400,000 is no longer controlled by the officials sheltered in buildings guarded by tommy guns of the blue-uniformed riot troops. . . ." The *New York Times* (June 15, 1962, p. 3) stated that on the eve of Algerian independence, thousands of *colons* were persuaded by terror and by fear to move to France daily. Between June 1 and June 12, for example, as many as 92,000 abandoned Algeria.

14. See *El-Moudjahid*, January 29, 1961. According to an inquiry made by the Club Jean Moulin, however, 300–400,000 *colons* would have to migrate if the problem of Arab urban unemployment was to be dealt with effectively. Class war would result if such repatriation did not take place, the authors concluded. It is said that de Gaulle agrees with these conclusions. See *L'Express*, January 19, 1961, pp. 22–23.

15. Frantz Fanon, *L'an V de la révolution algérienne* (Paris, 1959), pp. 177–178.

16. Such a possibility was partly contingent upon the treatment accorded to the 400–500,000 Algerians working in metropolitan France. These Algerians support about one-quarter of the total Moslem Algerian population financially. Their persecution or expulsion would doubtlessly inspire the FLN to reciprocate against the French *colon* population.

17. *Autour du drame* (Paris, 1961), p. 13.

18. The influence of Camus on Messadi's *As-Sud* (The Dam) was pointed out by Taha Hosseyn in a review in *Al-Jumhurriya* (Cairo), February 27, 1957. Messadi, it should be noted, has denied that his work reflects the negativism of *The Myth of Sisyphus*. See Lelong, *IBLA*, 20:239–268.

19. For example, Mohammed Dib, Mouloud Feraoun, Mouloud Mammeri.

20. *The Reporter*, November 28, 1957, pp. 37–39. Camus was interviewed

by Jean Bloch-Michel. Camus' friend Feraoun was brutally assassinated by members of the SAO on March 15, 1962, at Algiers.

21. In his short story, "L'hôte," Camus portrayed a man of good will who tries to reconcile, but is rejected by, both sides. Among those who were disappointed in Camus was his friend, also a liberal *colon*, Jean Daniel. Daniel felt Camus should at least have continued to bear "witness" by writing about Algeria, thus helping to prepare for a day of reconciliation between Arabs and French. See *L'Express*, January 7, 1960, pp. 27–29. Similar disappointment was expressed by Jules Roy in his *La guerre d'Algérie* which was dedicated to the memory of Camus. Roy, in 1960, believed the only solution to the war was the creation of an Algerian republic in which the French settlers would enjoy equal rights. Had Camus lived to revisit the Kabyle and see the horrors of the war, Roy believes, he would most probably have come to Roy's conclusions. Daniel, it should be observed, changed his mind about Camus in late 1961. The chaotic violence into which the Algerian problem had disintegrated by then led Daniel to ask whether Camus had not been right all along in his prediction that the use of terror as a tactic could only lead to anarchy. Perhaps, Daniel suggested, Camus' views on the Algerian question should be reconsidered and the judgment that Camus had been "too noble for 'the times'" revised. *L'Express*, January 19, 1962, p. 12. On a philosophical plane it was Jean-Paul Sartre who led the attack on Camus' moralistic stand. He accused Camus of tolerating evil by his refusal to combat it effectively, i.e., by "revolution."

22. Quoted in *La Nouvelle Critique* (January 1960), p. 68 fn. Malek Haddad in a talk in Beirut (June 16, 1961) spoke of Camus in almost the same terms as did Yacine.

23. *Education Nationale*, January 3, 1960, pp. 65–69.

24. Various interpretations have been made of *The Stranger*. Nora suggests that the novel might be seen as a fable of the isolation and meaninglessness of the *colon's* existence in a world increasingly alien to himself. The Arab whom Meurseult assassinates so violently (Meurseult fires five bullets) is the "unknown" and so the ominously dangerous adversary (*Les français d'Algérie*, pp. 190–192). Sartre in his pioneering interpretation of *The Stranger* in *Situations III* offered a metaphysical interpretation — Meurseult's situation is seen as the human situation as such.

25. *L'Algérie et la république* (Paris, 1958), p. 107.

26. Fanon observes, and Sartre in the preface to his book agrees, that terrorism and brutality are a necessary part of decolonization for psychological reasons. Only by a violent rejection of the colonizers, who once made him feel inadequate, can the colonized "'reconstruct his personality." *Les damnés de la terre*, p. 65.

27. Where *colons* have seemed to transcend their provincialism, as with Jules Roy for example, the emphasis in their solutions tends to be upon preserving the world of the *colons* but admitting the Arabs to brotherhood and equality. The emphasis among members of the FLN, on the other hand,

is upon an Arab Algeria in which *colons* can choose to live if they accept
its terms. The rebel Algerian novelist, Malek Haddad, has denied that Roy
in his "belated *mea culpa*" indicated that he would accept an independent
Algeria "whatever the consequences." Haddad's attitude toward Roy was
not wholly unjustified. Roy described his point of view in September 1961
in the following terms: "Certainly, for a long time now many of us have
thought that in the present world the independence of Algeria is not only
fated but is desirable for France. Not one of us, however, ever believed
that the force of French arms would not be replaced by the prestige of
the French mission or that the alliance of blood, of heart and of mind
would not replace our former dominance. For us, in any case, it can never
be a question of withdrawing [*dégager*] men or efforts." "Ce mot navrant"
in *L'Express*, September 14, 1961, p. 65. Nora, and Julien in the preface to
his book, express grave doubts as to the reality of *colon* "liberalism." They
do not, however, attempt to explain the case of the Frenchmen who have
identified themselves as Algerians and are fighting on the side of the FLN.
See Nora, *Les français d'Algérie*, p. 25 and chap. v.

28. See Robert de Montavalon, *Ces pays qu'on n'appellera plus colonies*
(Paris, 1956). During the protectorate Father André Demeerseman, director
of the White Fathers in Tunisia, hid Bourguiba from the French authorities
on one occasion. The President has stated, according to a reliable in-
formant, that so long as he remains in power, the Order will not be bothered
in any of its activities. But in the heyday of French imperialism, Lavigerie
identified the Catholic presence with the French presence and his organization did espionage work for the French government. See *Documents
Diplomatiques Français* 1.3:426–428 Algiers, April 11, 1881) in which
Lavigerie indicates that in expectation of French support in bringing Tunis
into the diocese of Algiers and so thwarting the Italian Capucins, he offered
the Director of Political Affairs of the Ministry of Foreign Affairs the full
services of his Order to defend and extend the French political presence.

29. *El-Moudjahid*, September 25, 1960, p. 10. Ferhat Abbas' recently
published *La nuit coloniale* (Paris, 1962) is in part dedicated to French
Leftists who aided the Algerian cause. This volume is the first one of a
projected three-volume study entitled *Guerre et révolution d'Algérie*.
Abbas states that he is writing this book with the hope that the truth might
"preserve the last chances of a loyal and fruitful cooperation between the
Algerian people and the French people."

CHAPTER V: "CULTURAL OPPRESSION" AND THE REJECTION OF ASSIMILATION

1. *La Tunisie* (Paris, 1951), pp. 183 ff.
2. Albert Memmi, *Portrait du colonisé, précédé du portrait du colonisateur* (Paris, 1957); Malek Bennabi, *Vocation de l'Islam* (Paris, 1954).
3. *What is Algeria?* (November 1956).
4. This speech was originally given at the Congress of Afro-Asian writers

in Tokyo (March 1961). Excerpts of it were printed in *El-Moudjahid*, May 12, 1961, p. 12.

5. Allal al-Fassi, *The Independence Movements in Arab North Africa*, trans, H. Z. Nuseibeh (Washington, D.C., 1954), pp. 60 ff. For a discussion of French religious and political "oppression" in Morocco see Landau, *Moroccan Drama*, especially chap. ii entitled "The Berber Dahir." The Dahir of 1930, crucial in arousing both Moslem and nationalistic opposition to the French, was interpreted as an attempt to divide Berbers and Arabs by providing the former with a special judicial system of their own. For an over-all attack upon French "cultural oppression" in Algeria, see Saadia and Lakhdar, "L'aliénation colonialiste et la résistance de la famille algérienne" in *Les Temps Modernes* (June 1961), pp. 1680-1734. But this testimony in its extravagance is the sort of historical recreation which Julien and others have denounced as unscientific and even more dangerous than history written from the colonialist point of view because of the illusions it is likely to give newly independent people about their own history. See Nora, *Les français d'Algérie*, preface, p. 10.

6. Taillard, *Le nationalisme marocain*, pp. 95 ff.

7. These private schools received government aid after independence was won. They served 72,000 students in 1958.

8. Barbour, *A Survey of North West Africa*, 114 ff. For a discussion of the same claims and counterclaims, see Landau, *Moroccan Drama*, pp. 228-229, 235-236.

9. "Rapport à l'O.N.U. anné 1954-55: conditions de l'enseignement."

10. The French could have also argued that, in the early period of the protectorate, many of the politically articulate Tunisians — the so-called "Young Tunisians" — wanted a wholly French education for young Tunisians. In an interesting case in 1908, Ali Bach-Hamba, political editor of *Le Tunisien* (the paper of the Young Tunisians), attacked Khairallah Ben Mustapha (an eminent educationalist and political figure) for wanting the modernization rather than the suppression of the traditional *kuttab*. Bach-Hamba wanted the government to encourage only the French-Arab schools in which all the fundamental subjects were taught in French. See Chedly Khairallah, "Le mouvement jeune tunisien," in *Essai d'histoire et de synthèse des mouvements nationalistes tunisiens* (Tunis, n.d.) vol. I, pp. 141-142.

11. Barbour, *A Survey of North West Africa*, pp. 319 ff. Barbour feels that the French did an unusually good job in Tunisia in the sphere of education. But, *n.b.*, his figures include the non-Moslem children, most of whom went to school.

12. (Tunis, 1957), pp. 218 ff.

13. This school was founded in 1896 and offered a special education including modern science and French and Arabic languages. The opposition to its founding came, in part, from professors of the Great Mosque who felt that it would constitute a profanation of Islam. Tunisian modernists like Tlatli tended to accuse the French of submitting to pressure from the

traditionalists only to frustrate Tunisian progress. Thus, Tlatli believed, the French took a very long time before they permitted a certain amount of modernization to take place in the curriculum of Zaitouna with the excuse that "old traditions" should be respected.

14. Sadiqi, according to a French authority, was reorganized in 1892. It was given a French director and the curriculum was changed to provide more French courses that would allow a student to reach his *baccalauréat*, first part. It served, in its reformed state, as both a training school for future officials of the beylical service and translators, and to help "create, at the same time, a Moslem intellectual elite open to European culture." Yves Chatelain, *La vie littéraire et intellectuelle en Tunisie de 1900 à 1937* (Paris, 1937), p. 27. In spite of this, energetic professors of Arabic managed to inspire their students with a love for Arabic culture and literature. Among these dedicated teachers were Ali Behaouone, Abdelwahab Bakir, and Mahmoud Messadi. See Josette Ben Braham, "Sadiki. . ." in *Afrique-Action*, February 20, 1961, pp. 14–15.

15. André Raymond indicates that, in 1955, 77 per cent of the Europeans were in school (94 per cent of the French), while only 30 per cent of the Moslems were in school (225,000). And this was after the French had decided to speed up their campaign to increase enrollment (in 1950). *La Tunisie*, p. 53.

16. "Essential Notions about Algeria" (Paris), edited by *Le Gouvernement Général d'Algérie*.

17. Algiers is the third largest French university in the world.

18. Barbour, *A Survey of North West Africa*, pp. 237 ff. For the educational backwardness of Algeria, the *colons* are particularly responsible. They consistently sought to curb metropolitan efforts to extend education to the Arabs and to frustrate the teaching of the Arabic language. See C.-H. Favrod, *La révolution algérienne* (Paris, 1958). Among the interesting statistics given in Favrod's book are these: in 1954 there was one European student for every 227 Europeans in Algeria while there was only one Moslem student for every 15,342 Algerian Moslems. In the same year there were 99 Moslem Algerian doctors, 161 lawyers, 185 teachers, 28 engineers of various sorts. Of the 2,500 government functionaries in Algeria, only 183 were Moslems and most of these were janitors and doormen. Nora observes that the fact the *colons* allowed the Arabs any education at all shows their lack of a historical sense:: "A historical view of colonization would have carefully barred the access of Moslems to culture" (*Les français d'Algérie*, p. 217).

19. The number of Moslems in elementary schools increased, between 1957–58 and 1959–60, from 350,835 to 625,013 according to an official French statement. *New York Times*, October 30, 1960, sect. 11, p. 9.

20. Julien, *L'Afrique du Nord en marche*, p. 38. Observers of the Belgrade Conference in August 1961 were interested to note that the new president of the GPRA, Ben Youssef Ben Khedda, addressed the conference in French.

See *Le Monde*, September 6, 1961, p. 2. Julien, p. 39, testifies to the fact that the North African *évolués* learned French quite thoroughly. He cites A. Berque in *Les intellectuels algériens* as having come to the same conclusion.

21. T. Brady, *New York Times*, September 29, 1957.

22. "Quatre générations, deux cultures" in *La Nouvelle Critique* (January, 1960), pp. 29–49.

23. *Le jeune algérien*, pp. 61–62, 99, 128, 138, 143–144.

24. Quoted in H. Goldberg, *French Colonialism: Progress or Poverty?* (New York, 1959). The article first appeared in Abbas' paper *L'Entente*, February 23, 1936. Maunier, *The Sociology of Colonies*, vol. I, pp. 398 ff., quotes an Algerian Berber intellectual as saying: "Islam is a death factor; we must therefore secularize"; and other *évolués* are cited to the same effect. The Moroccan novelist, Driss Chraibi, gives a vivid portrait of the *évolué* as an "angry young man" in rebellion against the traditions of his family and of the *medina* in *Le passé simple* (Paris, 1955). At one point in his youth the protagonist of the novel tells his father that he wants to live now rather than wait for an imaginary future life in heaven. The father answers caustically: "So monsieur cannot wait? . . . And to think that you were once our pride! We used our old babouches so that you could have a pair of new shoes, and we almost starved ourselves so that you could be what we expected. And what have you done. . . ? Blithely you walk into the European city. . . ." (p. 27).

25. Michel Devèze, *La France d'outre-mer: de l'empire colonial à l'union française, 1938–1947* (Paris, 1948), pp. 32, 38–39. The Association of the Reformist Ulema of Algeria, inspired by the teachings of Muhammad Abdu, Al-Afghani, and Rashid Rida, was most probably not involved in the uprising of November 1, 1954. It was only in 1956 that it encouraged its members to cooperate with the FLN, and most of the leaders of the FLN were modernists rather than religious reformists. See Jacques Carret, "L'association des Oulema réformistes d'Algérie" in *L'Afrique et l'Asie*, no. 43 (1958). A group of assimilated modernists similar to those in Algeria existed in Tunisia before World War II. This group included Mohammed Nomane and Mahmoud Aslan who were novelists, and Tahar Essafi, an essayist, who went so far as to advocate mixed marriages between Europeans and Moslems as a method of modernizing. Nomane was particularly hostile to traditional Islam and saw the modern French *lycée* as the gateway to progress. See Chatelain, *Le vie littéraire*, pp. 125–126, 154–155.

26. "France and Islam," *Foreign Affairs* (July 1940), pp. 680–699.

27. Brunschwig, *La colonisation française*, p. 81. In 1946, Abbas defended a program which would have made Algeria an autonomous state with its own flag but a common foreign policy with France. Algerians and French would enjoy full rights of citizenship in the other's territory and French as well as Arabic would be the official languages of Algeria. See *L'Express*, January 26, 1961, pp. 3–4.

28. Paul Emile Sarrasin, *La crise algérienne* (Paris, 1949), annexes, p. 220. For an account of how Messali Hadj's long imprisonment and apparent vanity cost him the leadership of the revolutionary movement see Jean Lacouture, "Messali Hadj et Ferhat Abbas. . . ." in *Le Monde*, *650* (March–April, 1961), p. 4.

29. Jean Lacouture, *Cinq hommes et la France* (Paris, 1961), p. 301. According to Lacouture, Abbas finally abandoned the idea of assimilation in 1942.

CHAPTER VI: ANTI-FRENCH LITERATURE IN FRENCH

1. See *La Nouvelle Critique* (January 1960), which is a special issue devoted to Algerian culture; Jean Bloch-Michel, "Paris Letter," *Partisan Review* (Winter 1959), pp. 95–99; and Marie Susini, "Naissance d'une littérature de combat" in *Etudes Meditérranéennes* (Spring 1960), pp. 67–72. A French writer, André Rétif, wrote in 1956 that the recent North African novels were very disturbing because in them little place was made for Europeans or assimilated Arabs and no mention was made of the dams, model farms, etc., with which the French had equipped Algeria. But, even though these novels were often "irritants et négatifs," they deserved considerable attention. See "La leçon des romans Nord-Africains" in *L'Afrique et l'Asie*, no. 33 (1956), pp. 20–22. Henri Kréa, in *Afrique-Action*, December 19, 1960, p. 22, makes the point that the Algerian intellectuals of 1954 having been denied a knowledge of Arabic in their education were forced to resort to French as the weapon to use against France. Malek Haddad, in the lecture referred to above, talked of French as "ma seule arme de combat."

2. Yacine's novel *Nedjma* (Paris, 1956) deals with the quest of a group of young Algerians for the identity of a beautiful and mysterious woman. Marie Susini in her survey of the contemporary school of Moslem Algerian writers, states: ". . . it is above all with Kateb Yacine that we find the fatherland: *Nedjma* (1956) the symbol itself of Algeria. . . ." *Etudes Méditerranéennes*, p. 71.

3. The third volume, *Le métier à tisser* (Paris, 1957), pictures Omar's life as an apprentice to a weaver in Tlemcen, 1940.

4. Also concerned with the dilemmas of the Algerian *évolué* are two other of Haddad's novels which are set mainly in Paris. Each deals with a futile and unhappy love affair between an Algerian writer and a French woman who seems to symbolize the seductiveness of French life. These novels are *Le Quai aux Fleurs ne repond pas* and *Je t'offrirai une gazelle*.

5. The hero is educated at a school of the *Alliance Israélite Universelle*, an organization helped by the French government and which continues to teach the French system and language in many parts of the world.

6. A criticism sometimes made by Frenchmen of these writers is that they tend to make systems out of their personal rancors and frustrations.

See the review of Mammeri's book in *IBLA*, 20:59–60 (1957) by J. Ballet. Memmi was described to the present author as being a man whose bitterness was in large part the product of his failure to pass his *agrégation*. He was so described by a French cultural officer in Tunisia. "P.R." writes of Memmi's *Portrait du colonisé*, in *L'Afrique et l'Asie*, no. 44 (1958), pp. 63–64, that it is often cruel and unjust, that one sees while reading it the "rictus douloureux" of the author, but that in spite of the fact that it will exasperate many, it is an interesting symptom of a certain type of mentality.

7. *Portrait du colonisé*, p. 146.

8. In *La Nouvelle Critique* (January 1960), p. 80.

9. *Afrique-Action*, January 23, 1961, p. 3.

10. *Afrique-Action*, February 13, 1961, p. 9.

11. See Michel Lelong in *IBLA*, 18:273–278 and his article "Culture arabe et culture occidentale dans la Tunisie d'aujourd'hui (Une enquête de la revue *Al-Fikr*) in *IBLA* 19:313–331 (1956). Several Tunisians who answered the periodical's questionnaire on culture denied that anything should be made of a distinction between Western and Oriental cultures. Sartre ended this issue of *Al-Fikr* by expressing the hope that a close cooperation between Maghreb and French culture would continue to be a reality. Similar sentiments were expressed by North African intellectuals at the International Seminar of North African Culture held in Tunis between August 16–19, 1957 (see *IBLA* 20:283–288 [1957]). While "cultural oppression" was condemned, a profound attachment to Western, and especially French, culture was expressed.

12. *Tunisie: sève nouvelle*, p. 213.

13. *Problèmes d'édification du Maroc et du Maghreb: quatre entretiens avec El-Mehdi Ben Barka* (Paris, 1949), pp. 34–35. The interviewer and editor was Raymond Jean.

14. *La Nouvelle Critique* (January 1960), p. 94. Charles Gallagher appears to share the author's conviction that French culture in the Maghreb is by no means doomed. He has observed that the succession of Hassan II, who is eminently frenchified, to Muhammad V "is the substitution of a biculture for a monoculture. It is evolutionary progress. . . ." American Universities Field Staff *Reports* 3.3:8 (Morocco, April 1961). Elsewhere he observes that what distinguishes North African from Middle Eastern culture is the former's "underlying Berber strangeness and its heavy overlay of European civilization." American Universities Field Staff *Reports* (Tunisia, November 1957).

CHAPTER VII: AMBIVALENT ATTITUDES OF EVOLUÉS AND THE PROBLEM OF IDENTITY

1. Fanon believed such symbols implied that only the colonizer, not the colonized, could make history and so was worthy of immortalization. "World of compartmentalization," wrote Fanon of the colonial world, "manichaean, immobile, a world of statues: the statue of the general who

has made the conquest, the statue of the engineer who has constructed the bridge. . . ." (*Les damnés de la terre*, p. 40).

2. According to Rom Landau, Abdallah Ibrahim, one-time premier of Morocco, believes that the beautiful Almohade ramparts of Rabat will have to be torn down some day. At present, Ibrahim told Landau, these walls cut the *medina* off from the modern city and so condemn the inhabitants of the *medina* to unsanitary conditions. Ibrahim went so far as to add that he considered the traditional past, and even Islam, a hindrance to progress. See *Morocco Independent*, pp. 76–79.

3. Bennabi, *Vocation de l'Islam*, argues the thesis that the Arabs were conquered by the French, in large part, because Arab culture had become uncreative and unable to defend itself.

4. An extreme example of this type of sympathetic but repressive exoticism is the attitude toward Morocco expressed by Pierre Loti: for Loti the beauty of Morocco lay in the "sound of the little African flutes, of the tam-tams and the iron castanets. . . . As to his majesty, the Sultan, I am glad that he is handsome; that he will have neither press nor parliament, roads nor railroads in his dominions; that he rides splendid horses, and that he made me a present of a long silver-mounted musket and a great sword inlaid with gold. . . . Let us live in a vague dream of eternity, careless of what earth has in store for us tomorrow. Let us grasp, as they pass, those things which do not deceive: beautiful women, fine horses, magnificent gardens and the perfumes of flowers. . . ." This passage appears in *Into Morocco*, trans. E. Robins (New York, 1892), pp. 5–8.

5. An example of repressive paternalism was the attitude of the one-time Resident-General in Morocco, General Guillaume. Referring to "the Moroccans who were educated in Paris and who have made intimate contact with our ideas of Liberty, Equality, and Fraternity," he once told an interviewer, "they . . . wish to leap over centuries without yet having found their own center. The Moroccans want too much, too much from us and too much from themselves. They can only become partners very slowly. . . ." This statement appears in Gisela Bonn, *Neue Welt am Atlas: was geht vor in Morokko, Algerien, Tunesien?* (Wiesbaden, 1955), pp. 80–82.

6. Messali Hadj, Abbas, and Bourguiba are, or have been, married to French women.

7. Gibb states the problem in the following way: ". . . the 'nation' is not something to be made — it is there, with all its heritage of history, of symbolisms, of emotional ties and attitudes. If it is to be re-made, to 'become itself', it must be re-made in a way which will preserve those things which characterize it as a nation." H. A. R. Gibb, "Islam in the Modern World" in *The Arab Middle East and Muslim Africa*, ed. T. Kerekes (New York, 1961), pp. 9–26, 21.

8. An excellent summary of the problem of cultural identity among all of the newly-liberated nations appears in Emerson, *Empire to Nation*,

chap. viii. The Lebanese writer and editor, Georges Naccache, writes: "We Orientals with western culture live in a perpetual state of internal division." *Al-Afkar* (July 1961), pp. 14–16. The concept of the marginal man was first introduced by Robert Park. It is discussed in Everett Stonequist's *The Marginal Man: A Study in Personality and Culture Conflict* (New York, 1937). In the introduction to this volume, Robert Park observes that while the marginal man suffers from self-consciousness because of his inability to feel comfortable in either one of two cultures, he can have the advantage of a broader horizon and he can be more "rational" and detached than the person who is fully adjusted to one culture. For a brief but illuminating discussion of the contemporary "marginal man" in Algeria, see Pierre Bourdieu, *Sociologie de l'Algérie* (Paris, 1958), pp. 90–126. For a discussion of the problem of the marginal man in North Africa generally, see Benjamin Rivlin, "Cultural Conflicts in French North Africa," *The Annals* 306:4–9 (July 1956), and Roger Le Tourneau, "North Africa: Rigorism and Bewilderment" in *Unity and Variety in Muslim Civilization*, ed. G. E. von Grunebaum (Chicago, 1955), pp. 231–254. Rivlin employs the term "cultural schizophrenia" to designate the condition of the North African marginal man. The problem of the marginal man in the Arab world is also discussed in Albert Hourani, *Syria and Lebanon* (London, 1946), pp. 70–72; Hisham Sharabi, "The Crisis of the Intelligentsia in the Middle East," *The Muslim World* 47:187–193 (1957); and Lelong, *IBLA* 19:313–331 (1956).

9. According to Lorna Hahn, *North Africa: Nationalism to Nationhood* (Washington, D.C., 1960), p. 16. While in Cairo during the struggle for independence, Bourguiba found that he was psychologically and morally a stranger among the eastern Arabs. He was especially unimpressed with the educational system of modern Egypt. See Lacouture, *Cinq hommes et la France*, p. 142.

10. See Charles Gallagher, "Looking Backward and Forward: Summing up the Situation in Morocco," American Universities Field Staff *Reports* 1:4 (Morocco, August 20, 1960). C.-A. Julien states in *Histoire de l'Afrique du Nord: Tunisie, Algérie, Maroc*, 2 vols. (Paris, 1951–52), vol. I, p. 49: "Les civilisations successives qui venaient du dehors ont été pour le Berbère autant de vêtements divers sous lesquels son corps et son âme demeuraient identiques à eux-mêmes." The French, however, were unsuccessful in their attempt to exploit the Berber-Arab dichotomy. For this failure a French Berberologist blames General Lyautey: ". . . under the impulse of Lyautey, the French succeeded in accomplishing what the Sultan had attempted without success. This was the unification of arabophone and berberophone Morocco. But they wished to do this in their own interest, while we accomplished it against ours." G. H. Bousquet, *Les Berbères* (Paris, 1957), pp. 71–72. Berbers in modern North Africa constitute 40–45 per cent of Morocco and 30 per cent of Algeria. The number of Berbers in Tunisia is

minimal. The term Berber designates a people who speak a language, not a people constituting a race or a self-conscious nationality.

11. See Le Tourneau in *Unity and Variety in Muslim Civilization* and Rivlin, *The Annals* 306:4–9. One of the fundamental principles of Mustafa Kemal Atatürk's revolutionary and nationalistic movement after World War I was "laicisation."

12. Gallagher, *Reports* 1:4.

13. Charles Gallagher, "Ramadan in Tunisia," American Universities Field Staff *Reports* 6:1 (Tunisia, April 5, 1960).

14. These problems are, of course, not unique to Arabs. Investigations of the *évolué* problem in India (E. Shils, *The Intellectual between Tradition and Modernity* [The Hague, 1961]), and in Black Africa (*Deuxième congrès des écrivains et artistes noirs* [Rome, 26 Mars–1er Avril, 1959]) reveal the same concern with the questions of language, identity, and unity.

15. Le Tourneau in *Unity and Variety in Muslim Civilization*. It should be observed that this discomfort with traditional Islam is presumably less true of those of the elite who have been educated both in the traditional koranic system and in Western universities. A study in contrast between the latter group and the purely French educated is E. Gellner, "The Struggle for Morocco's Past," *The Middle East Journal* (Winter 1961), pp. 79–90. Douglas Ashford, *Political Change in Morocco* (Princeton, 1961), p. 388, observes that the fact of being French educated does not assure, at least in Morocco, that *évolués* share the same political opinions. Culturally, however, he sees a sharp distinction between the French-educated Moroccans and those educated in traditional schools. While in the case of Tunisia the predominance of the Westernized *évolué* over the traditionalist and Moslem reformist in the latter stages of the nationalistic movement is clear-cut, this is not so of Morocco. In Morocco, the nationalistic movement has been inspired and directed by Westernized *évolués* and traditionally-educated Moslem reformists in almost equal measure. This is one reason why the tensions, with liberation, are greater in Morocco than in Tunisia. See Ashford, *Political Change in Morocco*, chap. ii.

16. For an example of a progressive's point of view in Morocco, see Ahmed Balafrej, "Morocco Plans for Independence," *Foreign Affairs* 34.3:483–489 (April 1956). And for the moderate Kemalist spirit of the leaders of Tunisia, see *Bourguiba Addresses the Nation's Leaders* (speeches of February 6 and 8, 1961) issued by the Secretary of State for Information. Balafrej writes that Islamic principles ". . . are in no way incompatible with the development of the world or with modern trends. On the contrary . . . the *ijtihad* — the interpretation of these principles — allows the commentators to adapt the principles of the Koran to the requirements of evolution and progress." Bourguiba said in his speech of February 8 much the same. He insisted that ". . . the Moslem religion is not a doctrine of intellectual asphyxia." The problem of the progressives is to convince the

conservative Ulema and their followers, among other things, that *ijtihad* is really "open," contrary to the orthodox view. See Rivlin, *The Annals* 306:4–9, and Le Tourneau in *Unity and Variety in Muslim Civilization*. Rom Landau describes the Ulema of the important Islamic center of Qarawiyin as being very upset by the process of educational modernization in independent Morocco. He cites as examples of their conservatism their view that the study of Islamic philosophy is too controversial a subject and that a new law disallowing parents to marry their daughters to very old men is against Moslem law. But Landau describes these Ulema as belonging to a lost generation. See *Morocco Independent*, pp. 241–245. For sources on early modernism in Tunisia, see Khairallah in *Essai d'histoire et de synthèse des mouvements nationalistes tunisiens*. Raymond, in *La Tunisie*, observes that the reformism of the Tunisian elite makes use of the symbols and terms of Islam and is not purely secularist as was the reformism of Mustafa Kemal Atatürk.

17. The author owes to Charles Gallagher the observation that while an educated Middle Easterner will invite one to an Arabic meal with naturalness, his North African counterpart will tend to look upon the meal as something of an exotic adventure, a common departure from one's customary European diet. Jean Daniel, in Tunis during the Generals' revolt in April 1961, was astonished at the deeply emotional way in which the Tunisians identified themselves with de Gaulle's cause. He implies that the identification went well beyond the natural anxiety the Tunisians had for the security of their own country. *L'Express*, April 27, 1961, pp. 17–18. Thomas Brady reports that when the Moroccan and Tunisian units serving with the United Nations first entered the Congo in 1960 their reaction was to feel like Europeans in the context of sub-Sahara Africa. Brady quotes a Tunisian officer as having said: "I ran into a very evolved Congolese today. He spoke extremely good French. . . ." *New York Times*, August 15, 1960.

18. Messadi's poetic drama *The Dam* is regarded generally as the most important literary product of modern Tunisia. This work reflects French existentialist thought, but it is written in high classical Arabic.

19. How little literature of real importance Tunisia produces is indicated in a survey of Tunisia in 1960 in *Afrique-Action*, January 2, 1961, pp. 14–15.

20. Rom Landau found that a group of Rabat notables, whom he interviewed, were very preoccupied with the problem of culture in Morocco. They maintained that the Moroccan problem was more complex than was the case in Tunisia and Algeria, paradoxically, because the French had only planted their culture superficially in Morocco. As a result, they stated, many Moroccan *évolués* tended to think in Arabic in spite of the excellence of their French, and Morocco had failed to produce writers of French expression like Malek Haddad and Kateb Yacine of Algeria. The notables revealed the confusion of the cultural situation, however, by denying to Driss Chraibi, the major Moroccan novelist of French expression, the right to call himself a Moroccan. According to them, Chraibi's "aestheticism"

and his antagonism to Moroccan and Islamic ways struck no chords in the hearts of the Moroccans. See Landau, *Morocco Independent*, pp. 56–60.

CHAPTER VIII: THE SEARCH FOR IDENTITY:
ARABIZATION AND MODERNIZATION IN NORTH AFRICA

1. In 1956, Morocco had only one *agrégé d'arabe* according to Vincent Monteil, *L'arabe moderne* (Paris, 1960), p. 100.

2. The director of the *Institut d'Etudes et de Recherches pour l'Arabisation* in 1960 was Ahmed al-Ahdar whose simplified system of Arabic script has been adopted by the government and made use of in school manuals. Al-Ahdar has described the language problem facing Morocco today in the following terms: ". . . Classical Arabic remains the tool of the educated. Dialectical Arabic remains the language of all. French is the language of modern progress. The ruling elite therefore speaks three languages (I pass over Berber in silence), without really possessing any one. . . . Conversation between bilingualists is automatically in French as soon as the subject of conversation reaches a certain level and becomes technical." In *Al-Istiqlal*, March 14, 1959, and quoted in Monteil, *L'arabe moderne*, pp. 357–358.

3. These figures appear in Landau, *Morocco Independent*, pp. 41–42. These figures do not include students studying in the schools of the Cultural Mission, the largest French Mission overseas.

4. It is true that in 1958, because of a shortage of Arabic teachers, the program of arabization had to be temporarily halted. The government decided to have science and mathematics taught in French and to limit the first two years of primary instruction to French (except for religious instruction). In 1958, also, the number of students admitted to school was about half of the number admitted in 1956. See Ashford, *Political Change in Morocco*, pp. 388–389, and Charles Gallagher, "Morocco Goes to School" in American Universities Field Staff *Reports*, 4.7 (Morocco, September 1958).

5. According to article 14 of the "Fundamental Law of Morocco": "The State must provide education, which has an Arab and Islamic national orientation and which suits the needs of the nation, including technical, professional and scientific training." See *The Middle East Journal* (Summer 1961), pp. 326–328, for the official text.

6. Almost symbolically, the large white structure with its arched facade, overlooks Government Square. An article on Sadiqi in *Afrique-Action*, February 20, 1961, pp. 14–15, is entitled "Sadiqi ou comment on devient ministre." Bourguiba, it might be added, transferred from Sadiqi to the Lycée Carnot to complete the final years of his secondary education.

7. *La Documentation Tunisienne*, June 25, 1958.

8. The facts and figures that follow were provided with great generosity by the Tunisian Ministry of Education. The documents made use of were:

Nouvelle conception de l'enseignement en Tunisie (October 1958) (which is an official elaboration of the principles of Bourguiba outlined in his speech to the graduates of Sadiqi); *A Ten Year Prospect of School Attendance; Study of the Creation of the Tunisian University* and *New Conception of Education in Tunisia.*

9. The following discussion excludes the French Cultural Mission Schools discussed in Chapter III. An officer of the French Cultural Mission told the author he was confident that for a long time French would be the predominant language (including Arabic) in government primary and particularly secondary schools for all modern subjects. He observed that the official statistics of the government tend to disguise this fact for political reasons, but that the educators of the country believe that the continued use of French as the basic medium of instruction in modern subjects is necessary.

10. Michel Lelong, "Une important réalisation tunisienne: la réforme de l'enseignement," *IBLA* 21:297–320 (1958).

11. This estimate appears in *A Ten Year Prospect of School Attendance* (Secretary of State for National Education).

12. *La Documentation Tunisienne*, October 4, 1960, pp. 3–9. About 18 per cent of the Tunisian budget is devoted to education. Some revealing figures were published in *La Dépêche Tunisienne*, February 26, 1961, for the year 1960–61. The increase of school enrollment over the previous year was 10 per cent. Of the 489,744 students now in school, 90 per cent were in primary school and the remainder in secondary (no figures were given for higher education). The number of Moslems in school was 461,000 (315,000 boys and 146,000 girls); the number of Jews was 8,000 (the boys and girls are about the same); and the number of Europeans was 23,924. The number of students in public education was 445,110; the number in schools of the *Mission Universitaire et Culturelle Française* was 32,088 (of these 8,080 were Moslems and 6,655 were Jews); and the number of students in the free Catholic schools was 12,546 (of whom 6,179 were Moslems and 713 were Jews). Of the Moslem students in free Catholic schools, 4,327 were girls.

13. This degree equipped a student, under the Protectorate, for a few administrative positions that did not require a modern education, or for higher studies in traditional Islamic fields.

14. Raymond, *La Tunisie*, pp. 100–101, gives the much lower figure for students at the Great Mosque (in 1959) of 372. By 1959, in any case, this famous medieval school was being transformed into little more than a school of theology.

15. Michel Lelong, "Situation de l'enseignement supérieur en Tunisie," *IBLA*, 23:77–85 (1960). (It is interesting to note that in 1958–59 courses in the Institute were taught by 53 French teachers, 12 Tunisians and one Belgian.)

16. In a letter to *Afrique-Action*, September 23–29, 1961, p. 2, a teacher

from metropolitan France expressed astonishment that French played so preponderant a role in the Tunisian educational system. She criticized the Tunisians for laziness in not making the effort to teach technical subjects, history, and geography in Arabic.

17. *Ibid.*, p. 1. See the great interest excited by the Lebanese lexicographer, Hanna el-Fakhouri, when he visited Tunis. *Afrique-Action*, January 23, 1961, p. 13.

18. See *IBLA* 23:1–6, 98–102 (1960).

19. See *IBLA* 19:415–422 (1956) for an account of the inquiry edited by Mahmoud Mamouri for *Ash-Shabab* (Tunis).

20. Demeerseman speaks of modernization as the "idée force" of the present elite and Gabriel Ardant (*La Tunisie d'aujourd'hui et de demain*, Paris, 1961) of the "volonté de modernisation." In *Esprit* (June 1957), Ahmed Ben Salah rejected the idea that decolonization should seek to reverse colonization. Rather, he stated, it should build upon and transform the modern structures colonization has already provided. For a portrait of Bourguiba as a modernist, see Lacouture, *Cinq hommes et la France*, chap. ii. Kemalist steps in Tunisia have included abolition of the rich religious foundations (the *habous*), of polygamy (and women can now divorce as easily as men), and campaigns have been waged against fasting at Ramadan and against wearing the veil.

21. The author is J. Ben Braham, April 3, 1961, p. 13.

22. When school opened, the fate of the Cultural Mission had not yet been decided. Of the some 945 French teachers on contract to the Tunisian government, 608 had returned to their posts at the request of the *Association Professionnelle des Enseignants Français en Tunisie*. This organization took the attitude that these contracts had been repudiated by neither the Tunisian nor the French government during the crisis of Bizerte and so were still in force. See *Le Monde*, October 11, 1961, p. 6. By the end of October the French government had ordered the teachers of the Cultural Mission to regain their positions, but the Mission itself would not be revived in Tunisia. Instead, these teachers would come under a special Cultural Section of the French Consulate. The operation of the new mission would be more closely supervised by the Secretary of State for Education and any new recruitment of students would be discouraged. See *Afrique-Action*, October 25–31, 1961, p. 13 and *Le Monde*, October 21, 1961, p. 6.

23. *Afrique-Action*, October 14–20, 1961, pp. 6–8. Reflecting on the French presence in Tunisia after the events of July 1961, a Tunisian student made the following remark: "To date we have assumed that there is no alternative but to co-operate with France indefinitely. The University of Tunis was little more than a French provincial university. One had to go to France to receive the doctorat, to do research, to specialize. The principle of bilingualism seemed untouchable and a priority was given to French over all other living languages." Another student added: "In brief, we have been at France's mercy. A shift in politics, an incident, and the formation

of our cadres is compromised. Well, no! All this must be changed." In
Afrique-Action, August 26–September 1, 1961, p. 11.

24. The spokesman was Carmel Tabone, a one-time lawyer in Tunisia.
See *Le Monde*, October 13, 1961, p. 7. The debate among Tunisian educators as to how to break the French educational monopoly appears in the
issues of *Afrique-Action* during the months of August, September, and
October, 1961. See, for example, Alya Daoud, "Les problèmes de la rentrée:
un instituteur raconte. . . .", *Afrique-Action*, October 7–13, 1961, pp. 14–15.
By December, 1961, the Tunisian government was taking steps to liberate
the economy, as well as the educational system, from the French hold.
Large private concerns like Phosphates of Gaza fell under considerable
government control. Europeans were required to hold work and trading
permits to do business in Tunisia, and these permits, renewable yearly, could
be revoked if Tunisians were available to replace the Europeans. Further-
more, the government was seeking capital from sources other than the
French — Switzerland and Italy in particular — to finance the new triennial
development plan. Although the process of economic liberation was, in the
Tunisian tradition, gradual and still based upon Western (if not French)
support, *Le Monde* (December 13, 1961, p. 6) concluded: "The colonial
economy is on its way to decolonization. . . ." See also *Jeune Afrique*,
December 13–19, 1961, p. 13.

25. Quoted in Barbour, *A Survey of North West Africa*, pp. 239–240.

26. It is often said that Ferhat Abbas cannot speak Arabic and that once
at a nationalist meeting he wept when it was suggested that as good nationalists all present should speak in Arabic. There is no doubt that French
is Abbas' language, but a U.S. State Department official tells of having heard
Abbas speak respectable Arabic at a social function, although after a while
he lapsed more comfortably into French.

27. The weekly of the FLN. The two editions are different. The Arabic
version tends to appeal to opinion and sentiment among Arab nationalists.
The French edition tends to be oriented toward liberal and radical opinion
in the West.

28. One-fourth of these 2,000 students were at the University of Algiers
— the rest were in France. The strike ended by the following academic
year.

29. Ten were in the new University of the Friendship of Peoples (Moscow) in 1960.

30. See Frantz Fanon's *L'an V de la révolution algérienne* for an understanding of the psychological and social results of the prolonged Algerian
war. Germaine Tillion in her *Les ennemis complémentaires* (Paris, 1960)
confirms that the war has tended to modernize Algerian society. Moslem
women, for example, serving as nurses or soldiers among the ALN, readily
abandon their veils. The French sociologist, Bourdieu, confirmed this in a
statement before the North-African Colloquium on Problems of Education
in the Maghreb. He observed that Algerians who had served in the *maquis*

were less traditionalist and more secular in their outlook than their compatriots, and that it would be from among these militants that their future elites of Algeria would come. He also stated that as a result of the experience of the revolution, the humblest peasant now wanted an education. See *France Observateur* (Paris), May 18, 1961, p. 16.

31. A. Guerard, *France: A Modern History* (Ann Arbor, 1959), p. 515. J. Gillespie, *Algeria: Rebellion and Revolution* (London, 1960), pp. 166–167 gives a critical analysis of the voting in the referendum as does Charles Gallagher in American Universities Field Staff *Reports* 4.6 (Algeria, September, 1958).

32. September 22, 1960, pp. 13–14. The reporter was Jean Daniel.

33. He was one of the *élus* called to Paris in 1960 to help de Gaulle formulate an administrative policy for Algeria.

34. The tragic and dramatic event of December 11–13, 1960 (when over one hundred Moslems were killed while expressing support for the FLN) was interpreted in France as conclusive proof that the myth of the FLN as only a minority terroristic organization, was dead. See *Le Monde, 634.* This was the interpretation of *El-Moudjahid* as one would expect. See issue of December 1960, p. 2. The extent to which urban Moslems abstained from voting in the Referendum of January 8, 1961, and the degree of participation in the strike of July 5, 1961, against partition, were similarly interpreted. Eighty deaths resulted from the strike in July. In an article in *Esprit* (January 1961), pp. 7–24, a group of anonymous officers gave testimony (and evidence) to the death of the myth of integration as preached by Jacques Soustelle *et al.*

35. See J. Daniel, *L'Express*, January 26, 1961.

36. "La France et l'Algérie" in *L'Express*, issues of December 22, 29 (1960) and January 4, 1961.

37. P. Herreman in *Le Monde, 641* (January–February 1961), p. 4.

38. Claude Krief concluded that Ben Khedda's appointment meant Algerians now wanted what an FLN leader called "the revolution of July 40." This is the combination of July 14 and of the Cuban July 26. Daniel in the same issue of *L'Express* interpreted the change in leadership to mean that the FLN had decided that the West could never allow real decolonization to take place. *L'Express*, pp. 5–67. This interpretation may have exaggerated the degree to which convictions of the leaders of the FLN had changed since 1954 and the extent of power that the relatively moderate Abbas had really ever held. The change of presidents, in short, may have had a tactical rather than an ideological significance. In any case, Ben Youssef Ben Khedda has been known for his radical views. In a revealing article in *El-Moudjahid*, January 5, 1961, p. 5, entitled "Impressions d'une tournée en Amerique Latine" he expressed some of these views. His tour of South America, he states, convinced him that the reason why South America was still relatively backward socially and economically, in spite of a century of independence, was that the early revolutionary leaders had failed to obtain complete inde-

pendence (economic as well as political) for their nations. Neo-colonialism had been allowed to continue in the form of economic exploitation. Algeria, he concluded, must avoid this possibility and press for a complete revolution that would resemble the revolution in Castro's Cuba. In Mexico he was impressed by General Cardena's statement: "Try to grasp for complete independence or it will take you another century to realize real independence, as with us Latin-Americans." French propagandists have claimed that if the FLN wins, Algeria would join the communist world. The present author believes that this is unlikely, that the tendency will be rather for the Algerians to identify with a radical pan-Arabism of the Egyptian variety. But, be that as it may, the Algerian rebels have, during the course of the revolution, moved progressively closer to the communist bloc. E. Behr observes that by 1962 one thousand members of the Algerian trade union (UGTA) will have received training in satellite nations. See *The Algerian Problem* (London, 1961), pp. 232–233. Ben Youssef Ben Khedda is nicknamed "Le Chinois" for having led the first Algerian mission to China. In 1960, Abbas himself went to Peking — even if he did so with a "heavy heart." *Le Monde, 642* (October 1960). The phrase is by "Sirius," the editor. Even before the autumn of 1960, Thomas Hodgkin, who visited behind the FLN lines, reported (*The Guardian*, October 6, 1960, p. 10): "I was driven in an East German car to watch Algerian girls making 80,000 pairs of pyjamas for their refugees with Czech sewing-machines out of Chinese cloth. The store-cupboards of the war orphans' homes were stocked with Russian flour and Chinese soap. I visited a rehabilitation centre which was being built with Yugoslav funds and will be staffed by Moslem doctors. The wounded, in serious cases, are transferred for specialist treatment to Eastern hospitals. Algerian doctors, engineers, economists are being trained — in considerable numbers — in Eastern universities." The title of this piece is "Algeria Turns against the West."

A major reason why the FLN has resorted to communist aid is that the Western powers, faithful to their French ally, have provided the Arabs with no aid and with little encouragement.

39. Devèze, *La France d'outre-mer*, p. 188.

CHAPTER IX: PROSPECTS — JULY 1962

1. *Afrique-Action*, February 13, 1961, pp. 8–9.

2. Paul Mus, *Le destin de l'union française: de l'Indochine à l'Afrique* (Paris, 1954), p. 25.

3. *Le Monde, 667* (July–August, 1961), pp. 1, 3.

4. *L'Express*, February 2, 1961, p. 36.

5. Robert Barrat, a liberal Catholic, who has closely and sympathetically followed and participated in North African affairs over a course of many years, believes that for the leaders of the FLN "it is not a matter of a xenophobic war against the West and against France, but rather of a poli-

tical struggle to end a politically, economically and socially oppressive regime." "Leaders of the FLN," he states, "have assured me on many occasions that the day that this form of domination disappears, nothing will prevent them from establishing the most sincere, loyal and fraternal of dialogues with France and with the French on the basis, of course, of equality and independence" ("Perspectives au-delà de la guerre" [a debate] in *Etudes Méditerranéennes* [Spring 1960], pp. 73–94, 88). This debate between authorities on North Africa includes many interesting statements as to the prospects for Algeria after the war has been ended.

6. The French presence remains a powerful factor in Lebanese life to a large extent because of the unusual composition of Lebanon. About 50 per cent of the population is Christian and insists upon maintaining close links with the West, the Maronites with France, in particular. See Eugène Mannoni, "Liban, dernier réduit de l'influence française au Proche-Orient" in *Le Monde, 456* (July 1957), p. 3. The title of this article written after the invasion of Egypt in 1956 by France (together with Britain and in probable alliance with Israel) summarizes the theme.

7. It is also true, of course, that in sub-Sahara Africa French (or English) will most probably remain the official language of the newly independent states for want of an alternative. It is often only in French that citizens of the French-speaking area can communicate with one another. See M. J. Herskovits, "Peoples and Cultures of Sub-Sahara Africa" in *The Annals* 298:11–20, 14 (March 1955).

8. The Algerian rebels tend to disparage the Moroccans and Tunisians for having settled for an independence which remains "neo-colonialist." By this they mean that the Moroccans and Tunisians are still subject to French economic and cultural control and are therefore not fully independent. A statement in *El-Moudjahid*, for example, reads: ". . . the French government has proven that it is more interested in a brutal hegemony, in prestige imposed by force, than in cooperation with the newly sovereign states. France does not take the independence of these states seriously." From an article in the issue of April 1958, p. 7, quoted in André Mandouze, *La révolution algérienne par les textes* (Paris, 1961), pp. 75–76.

9. Quoted in Mandouze, *La révolution algérienne*, p. 132, from *El-Moudjahid*, November 15, 1957.

DATE DUE

MAY 14 1965	JUN 0 9 1997		
OCT 2 6 1965			
NOV 12 1965			
DEC 3 1965			
JAN 19 1966			
MAR 15 1966			
MAY 2 0 1966			
JUN 12 1982			
DEC 16 1982			
DEC 17 1990			
APR 01 1991			
APR 22 1991			
SEP 1 1991			
APR 0 2 1995			
GAYLORD			PRINTED IN U.S.A.

Cultural Anthropology